W9-CBE-529

Your MONEY
in Tough Times

BARBOUR
PUBLISHING

© 2012 by Mahlon L. Hetrick

Print ISBN 978-1-61626-702-5

eBook Editions:
Adobe Digital Edition (.epub) 978-1-60742-872-5
Kindle and MobiPocket Edition (.prc) 978-1-60742-873-2

Churches and other noncommercial interests may reproduce portions of this book without the express written permission of Barbour Publishing, provided that the text does not exceed 500 words and that the text is not material quoted from another publisher. When reproducing text from this book, include the following credit line: "From *Your Money in Tough Times*, published by Barbour Publishing, Inc. Used by permission."

Scripture quotations marked KJV are taken from the King James Version of the Bible.

Scripture quotations marked NASB are taken from the New American Standard Bible, © 1960, 1962, 1963, 1968, 1971, 1972, 1973, 1975, 1977, 1995 by The Lockman Foundation. Used by permission.

Scripture quotations marked TLB are taken from The Living Bible © 1971. Used by permission of Tyndale House Publishers, Inc. Wheaton, Illinois 60189. All rights reserved.

Published by Barbour Publishing, Inc., P.O. Box 719, Uhrichsville, Ohio 44683, www.barbourbooks.com

Our mission is to publish and distribute inspirational products offering exceptional value and biblical encouragement to the masses.

 Member of the
Evangelical Christian
Publishers Association

Printed in the United States of America.

Contents

Introduction

This book was written to provide a simple, do-it-yourself budget workbook based on godly principles. The contents are derived from my thirty years of banking experience plus thirty years of counseling and teaching the Bible as a book of finance.

At this time of economic uncertainty, more and more individuals and families are seeking advice to help them make sound financial decisions. More and more radio and television programs are talking about solutions to our so-called money problems.

I believe that every problem has a solution and that God has the answer to every problem. The purpose of this book is to help you understand God's principles for managing money in a commonsense, practical way, and then to show you how to condense those principles into a budget.

Listening to God and obeying Him should result in greater joy, peace, and contentment in regard to your finances. The godly principles in this book have already helped hundreds of people become debt free, and thousands more are now working on their plans.

This book was written for all people who want to please God and bring glory to Him in every area of their lives, including the way they manage the possessions God has entrusted to them. It is also written for those who are struggling with finances, considering bankruptcy, or facing possible foreclosure, repossession, or suit.

We love you in the Lord, and our prayer is that we can help you experience God's best for you.

MAHLON L. HETRICK,
CHRISTIAN FINANCIAL COUNSELING, INC.

How to Find Abundance in Your Budget

"For the man who uses well what he is given
shall be given more, and he shall have abundance."
MATTHEW 25:29 TLB

GOD IS THE OWNER
For all the animals of field and forest are mine!
The cattle on a thousand hills. . . . for all the world
is mine and everything in it.
PSALM 50:10–12 TLB

GOD WANTS US TO ENJOY
For the earth and every good thing in it belongs to the Lord
and is yours to enjoy.
1 CORINTHIANS 10:26 TLB

MAN IS A STEWARD
Moreover it is required in stewards [manager],
that a man be found faithful [true].
1 CORINTHIANS 4:2 KJV

OUR PURPOSE IS TO GLORIFY GOD
If any man minister, let him do it as of the ability which
God giveth: that God in all things may be glorified.
1 PETER 4:11 KJV

TRUST GOD IN YOUR TIME OF TROUBLE
I want you to trust me in your times of trouble,
so I can rescue you and you can give me glory.
PSALM 50:15 TLB

EARN AN HONEST LIVING
If anyone is stealing he must stop it and begin using those hands of his for honest work.
Ephesians 4:28 TLB

HONOR THE LORD
Honour the LORD with thy substance, and with the firstfruits of all thine increase.
Proverbs 3:9 KJV

PAY YOUR TAXES
Render therefore unto Caesar the things which are Caesar's.
Matthew 22:21 KJV

GOD DEMANDS FAIRNESS
The Lord demands fairness in every business deal. He established this principle.
Proverbs 16:11 TLB

SAVE FOR THE FUTURE
The wise man saves for the future, but the foolish man spends whatever he gets.
Proverbs 21:20 TLB

Two Reasons for Saving:

1. Provide for Family: *But anyone who won't care for his own relatives when they need help, especially those living in his own family, has no right to say he is a Christian.*
1 Timothy 5:8 TLB

2. Give to Those in Need: *Let him that stole steal no more: but rather let him labour, working with his hands the thing which is good, that he may have to give to him that needeth.*
Ephesians 4:28 KJV

1.

Know Your Weaknesses: Identifying Money Problems

If your car won't start, you need to identify the problem and treat the cause before it can be solved. The same is true with your finances.

You know you are in financial bondage when:

- You are not putting God first with your tithe.
- You are borrowing to buy a want or a luxury.
- You are not able to pay all your bills on time.
- Your outgo exceeds your income.
- You do not have a balanced budget.
- You are receiving delinquent letters or phone calls.
- You are not saving for the future.
- You borrow from one lender to pay another lender.
- You are not being honest about your finances.
- You are using your reserves to pay for your overspending.

- Money problems are destroying your marriage.

These problems can often be traced back to two common issues: ignorance and wrong attitudes.

Ignorance

We went to school and learned all the skills to earn a living, but most of us were not required to take even one course on how to manage our money after we have earned it. We are not dumb, but we are ignorant. Based on your income, how much can you afford to spend for housing, food, transportation, insurance, entertainment, and so on? Many people don't know the answer to that question and don't even know where to go to get guidelines. You can graduate with a PhD in finance and not know how to put together, organize, analyze, and control a family budget.

Most people who think they have a budget are just record keepers. Some people are good record keepers, some are poor record keepers, and some don't even keep any records at all. A budget is a written plan to determine how income will be allocated in a proper balance to meet all one's needs and goals.

We are ignorant because we have not been taught. The Bible is the best book on finance ever written. God has more to say in the Bible about money than any other subject except love. But are we looking in the Bible for direction? Are we listening to God? If we don't know the Bible is the best book on finances ever written, we won't go to it for information or direction in money matters.

Wrong Attitudes

We are made up of two things: our attitudes and our actions. Great philosophers have said, "We become what we think." God says in Proverbs 23:7 (KJV), "For as he thinketh in his heart, so is he." We do what we think; our actions are a result of our thinking. We don't have a money problem—we have an attitude problem regarding money and money matters.

Specific attitude problems include:

Pride. "I am too proud to live in an old house, drive an old car, or wear old clothes. I want the nicest, newest, biggest, and best—whether I can afford them or not. After all, I don't want anybody to think I'm not successful." God says we are to be humble, not proud.

Greed. "I am going to get what I want. The world's attitude is 'whoever gets the most toys wins,' so I am going to gather my toys whether I can afford them or not." God says we are to be generous, not greedy.

Covetousness. "I want what other people have. I want to keep up with the neighbors, my peers, my family. I want to keep up with 'the Joneses.' " You don't have to worry about keeping up with the Joneses. I saw it on a very reliable source— an old episode of *The Flintstones*. Fred said the Joneses had just declared bankruptcy, so we don't need to worry about keeping up with the Joneses any longer. God says we should not covet what our neighbors have.

Lack of Discipline. Discipline is simply setting the rules and then following them. If we do not set rules based on our income and follow them, we are living within our credit. The average family in the United States is spending 122 percent of its income. Business failures have doubled in recent years due to businesses spending more money than they make. The government isn't innocent of overspending either. Since 1934, we have been spending more money than we receive in revenues. Individuals, families, businesses, and government entities are all going one way—the wrong way. God told us in Proverbs 21:20 (TLB), "The wise man saves for the future, but the foolish man spends whatever he gets." We are not wise (spending less than we get); we are not even foolish (spending everything we get); we are *more than foolish* (spending beyond our income). If we want to be wise, our goal should be to set a fixed spending level below our income and save whatever's leftover for the future.

Discipline. "Discipline" is a very positive word because it is necessary to reach our goals. Without discipline no athlete is a winner—that is, reaches the goal. Without discipline (rules and following the rules), we have no peace in the world. Without discipline (rules and following the rules), we have no education in the classroom. Without discipline (rules and following the rules), we have no safety on the highways. Why do we think we can earn and spend money with no rules, guidelines, or budget and still reach our goals? We can't. We must have the discipline of a written plan, a budget. Lack of discipline is a serious attitude problem. God says we are to save for the future, and the only way we can do that is to discipline ourselves to spend less than we receive. A budget helps us to do that.

Lack of Contentment. We are the most discontent, dissatisfied nation in the world. We want bigger, better, and more of the latest fashions, models, and styles. How do we know we are discontent? Did the family who bought their last house buy it because their old house was falling down or no longer livable? Did the person who bought his latest car buy it because his old car would not go one more mile and could not be repaired? Did the person who bought clothes recently buy them because all she had in the closet were rags and hangers?

It is very doubtful that is the reason they made their purchases. You see, we are not content, so we buy bigger, better, and more. Paul said in the New Testament that whether he had much or little, he was content (Phil. 4:11). God is telling us to be content with what He provides.

You Think You Owe It to Yourself. The new-car salesperson tells you, "You look great in that luxury coupe. You owe it to yourself. Go ahead and buy it." The salesperson in the exclusive dress shop tells you, "You look elegant in that $350 dress. You owe it to yourself. Go ahead and buy it."

If you listen to everyone who reassures you that, "You owe it to yourself," you'll quickly find out who you really owe it to—Visa, MasterCard, this bank, or that merchant, etc. Proverbs 21:2 (TLB) tells us, "We can justify our every deed but God looks at our motives." Are we simply trying to justify buying luxurious, extravagant items? God says we are to be diligent and wise managers, and to do what is right for the right reasons.

The world's way encourages us to be proud, greedy, covetous, and discontent, and to spend without discipline. We experience borrow-borrow, spend-spend, operate on other people's money, gain leverage, get easy credit, pay it back with cheaper dollars. When we listen to the world's ways and ignore God's ways, we have wrong attitudes that cause money problems.

The best way to prevent money problems is to adopt the following attitude: Use it up! Wear it out! Make it do! Or do without!

2.

It's Never Too Late: Finding Solutions

We can't get to where we are going until we know where we want to go. Setting goals is the first step toward reaching them. Most of us will have many goals—some immediate and short-range, others long-range for the future. Every Christian should set goals that bring glory to God and that meet personal and family needs.

Where do we start? Make a list of short-range goals that you want to accomplish this month or this year: for example, pay all bills on time, start a savings account, increase giving to God, and so on. Next, make a list of long-range goals: for example, save to replace a car in three years and pay cash for it; save for a down payment on a home; save for children's college education; provide adequate life insurance and health insurance; save for retirement; execute a will that honors God and provides for the family. Both short- and long-range goals will grow as you continue to revise the list. Proverbs 29:18 (KJV) says, "Where there is no vision [goals], the people perish."

We can know where we want to go, but we are not going to get there until we take action. Procrastination is the number-one reason for financial failure. One definition of success is "Do it now." We are to be "doers of the word, and not hearers only" (James 1:22 KJV). So let us get started doing those things that will lead us to being successful money managers for God.

Seven Steps for Good Money Management

Step 1: Set Goals and Make Plans

In Proverbs 16:9 (TLB), we read, "We should make plans—counting on God to direct us." A budget is a written plan to determine how the money that comes into the home is going to be allocated in a proper balance to honor the Lord, meet all our needs, and reach our goals. Everything should be in a proper balance with no frustration, worry, or fears about money. This plan should result in peace, contentment, and joy over money matters. Remember, if it doesn't work on paper, it will not work in reality.

Many times we have more dreams and goals than we can reach at one time. In our monthly budgets, we may run short of funds to accomplish everything in one month. When this happens, we need to look over our written list and establish priorities. A simple procedure could be to check off all the items that are absolute needs. Then as funds permit, add wants. Keep in mind that our first priority is to honor God. Then we are to meet our obligations to the government. And the balance—which we call "net spendable"—is the discretionary amount for us to allocate to the remainder of our budget items.

If and when circumstances change, we may need to modify our budget plan. When we receive a raise, we need to allocate where we are going to apply the additional funds in our budget. If we have an unplanned expense or we experience a reduced income, we need to reassess our expenditures. We may receive an inheritance, a large gift, or a big bonus: these are other reasons to modify our plan. Our overall goal should be to get out of debt and stay out of debt. Each modification should support that goal. Another goal should be to save for the future, so our modified plan should always include spending less than we have coming in so that we can have an abundance from which we can save for the future. The apostle Paul admonishes in Romans 13:8 (KJV), "Owe no man any thing." And Proverbs 21:20 (TLB) teaches, "The wise man saves for the future, but the foolish man spends whatever he gets."

Step 2: Trust God

God tells us in Proverbs 3:5–6 (KJV), "Trust in the LORD with all thine heart; and lean not unto thine own understanding. In all thy ways acknowledge him, and he shall direct thy paths." God said that if we meet the two prerequisites— place our trust in Him (not in ourselves, not in our understanding, but in His understanding) and acknowledge Him in all our ways (put God first in every area of our life, including finances), then He will direct our paths.

Step 3: Be Orderly

God says that He wants us to do all things in an orderly fashion. First Corinthians 14:40 (NASB) says, "All things must be done properly and in an orderly manner." That is what a budget helps us do.

Step 4: Gather Facts

Then God tells us to gather the facts: "What a

shame—yes, how stupid!—to decide before knowing the facts!" (Proverbs 18:13 TLB). God is warning us not to make a decision before we gather all the information we need to make a wise decision.

Step 5: Seek Counsel

If we still don't know what to do, we are to seek counsel. "Without consultation, plans are frustrated, but with many counselors they succeed" (Proverbs 15:22 NASB). In Psalm 1:1 (KJV), God cautions: "Blessed is the man that walketh not in the counsel of the ungodly." We are to seek counsel from the godly, those who follow God's ways and God's Word, if we want to be blessed.

Step 6: Commit

A commitment is a decision. When we have a choice of two options, we can't avoid making a decision. We must decide whether to follow the plan or not to follow the plan. If we don't follow the plan, our goals, visions, and dreams will never become real. God wants us to give our best and succeed, not give our second best and fail. One of the biggest problems in our society today is broken promises. Proverbs 16:3 (TLB) says, "Commit your work to the Lord, then it will succeed." And in Ecclesiastes 5:5 (TLB) we are cautioned, "It is far better not to say you'll do something than to say you will and then not do it."

We could know all the verses in the Bible, study them, memorize them, teach them, and even be hired as a consultant, but we still will not have solved one problem until we have commit ted our work to the Lord. Commit your work to the Lord today. Make a list of everything you possess, and then sign a statement saying, "I now transfer the ownership of everything back to God." Then pray the following:

> *Forgive me, Lord, for thinking I was the owner and acting like the owner. Now that I understand that You are the owner and I am the manager, just help me to manage in a way that brings glory to You. Help me to earn it honestly, honor You with the first part, give to the government, provide for my family, save for the future, help others in need, and then, Lord, help me to follow Your steps of being a good manager.*

It is at this point that I have seen lives changed and marriages on the rocks being brought back together. God has a lot of fringe benefits in store for us—love, joy, peace, and contentment—none of which we can buy. If we will only listen to Him and be obedient, He has blessings and prosperity in store.

What if a person decides to start managing money God's way and has a whole stack of bills that can't be paid? God tells us in Psalm 50:15, "I want you to trust me in your times of trouble, so I can rescue you" (TLB). Then in Proverbs 13:13, we see we have a choice: "Despise God's word and find yourself in trouble. Obey it and succeed" (TLB). To be successful we need to trust and obey God's word. Since many people worry over money troubles, God tells us in Matthew 6:34, "Don't be anxious (worried) about tomorrow. God will take care of your tomorrow too. Live one day at a time" (TLB). Simply put your worries in God's "worry basket." It appears that He is telling us to take it one day at a time, trusting and obeying Him. Stop worrying and leave the blessings up to Him.

Step 7: Obey God

In Proverbs 2:1–2 (TLB), God says, "Every young man who listens to me and obeys my instructions will be given wisdom and good sense." We derive two key questions from these verses: (1) "God, what are You telling us? We're listening"; (2) "What do You want us to do about it? You want us to obey Your instructions."

If we listen and obey, wisdom and good sense will be given to us, and most of financing is a matter of wisdom and good sense. God goes on to say, in verses 3 through 5, "Yes, if you want better insight [a better understanding of God's Word] and discernment [to know right from wrong], and are searching for them as you would for lost money or hidden treasure, then wisdom will be given you." We need to want insight and discernment; God will not force them on us. We need to be searching for insight in His Word. He is not going to drop a spiritual rock on our head and grant us all wisdom overnight. If we are searching for it and if we want it, wisdom and knowledge of God will be given to us.

We will get to know God for who He is— the almighty, all-merciful, all-forgiving, all-loving God. And when we get to know Him for who

He is, something will soon happen: "You will soon learn the importance of reverence for the Lord and of trusting him" (Proverbs 2:5 TLB). When we study God's Word and get to know Him better, we will gain trust and respect and reverence for God. Verse 6 adds, "For the LORD grants wisdom!" Wisdom comes from God. "His every word [the Bible] is a treasure of knowledge and understanding. He grants good sense to the godly—his saints. He is their shield, protecting them and guarding their pathway. He shows how to distinguish right from wrong, how to find the right decision every time. For wisdom and truth will enter the very center of your being, filling your life with joy" (vv. 6–10).

God gives us a promise. He tells us in Proverbs 16:20, "God blesses those who obey Him; happy is the man who puts his trust in the Lord" (TLB). God is saying that blessings and joy will be ours when we obey Him and put our trust in Him. And God keeps His promises!

3.

Biblical Insight:
Finding Abundance in Your Budget

Tragically, most people do not know how to find an abundance in their budgets, and they are going to the wrong source. They are not listening to what God has to say. If they turned to Matthew 25:29 (TLB), they would find that it says, "For the man who uses well what he is given shall be given more, and he shall have abundance." What Jesus is saying is that the man who manages well is the one who is going to have an abundance. Too often we listen to what the world says when we ought to be listening to God. Jesus does not say in this verse that the person who is born in the right home, has the right job, goes to the right school, lives in the right country, or is in the right place at the right time is the one who is going to have an abundance. He says, "For the man who uses well. . .shall have abundance."

As I said earlier, although we are taught skills to earn a living, most of us have not been taught how to manage money after we have earned it. We need to know the answers to questions such as these: What percentage of my budget can be spent for clothing? For food? For transportation? For entertainment? For housing? How much can I afford to spend in these various areas and have a balanced budget and be a good manager? Many of us don't even know where to get the answers to these questions. A person can graduate with a PhD in finance and still not know how to put together a family budget, analyze a budget, or set up a system of budget control. We send people into outer space, we have built a global audio and video communication system, yet we have failed to teach our families—God's first institution and the backbone of our nation—how to be good managers, which God says is the key to having an abundance.

We all seem to struggle along and learn from trial and error or from other people. Some of us even learn Thomas Edison's way—finding 999 ways how *not* to do something before we finally learn how to do it. Ultimately we continue to do the same thing over and over in an attempt to treat the symptoms of our money problems—not solve the problems.

Consider the parable of the talents in Matthew 25:14–30. To the first the master gave five talents, and the servant doubled it; to the second the master gave two talents, and the servant doubled it; to the third the master gave one talent, and the servant buried it. When the master returned, he said to the servant who turned five talents into ten, "Well done, good and faithful servant. Since you managed well, I will entrust to you more, and it will be a joyous task" (author's paraphrase). He said the same thing to the servant who had two talents and ended up with four. The master was not concerned with how much the servants had in the beginning, but with how well they managed whatever they had. And to the one who had one talent and buried it, he said, "Wicked man, lazy slave, at least you should have put the money in the bank and earned interest. Since you haven't done that, I'm going to take it from you and give it to the one who has the ten and knows how to manage" (author's paraphrase), and that is what he did.

What is Jesus teaching in this parable? In the beginning, He says the master gave different amounts according to the servants' abilities. Abilities to do what? To manage! God is not going to give everybody the same amount, so we should not be envious of people who have more;

nor should we look down on those who have less. It does not necessarily mean that one is in sin because he has less and the other is being blessed of God because he has more. That is not the case. If the amount of money and possessions we have are in direct relationship to our spiritual growth and obedience, then why were the disciples so poor, and why did Jesus have nothing but the clothing on His back? Let us be careful that we do not misunderstand. Yes, God does expect us to be good managers, but having material wealth is not an indication that we are spiritual or godly. We may be godly, but material wealth is not necessarily the only measure of this.

Jesus is also teaching that the way we manage determines whether we have joy. If we manage well, we will have more, and it will be a joy. If we blow it and mismanage, we will lose what we have. God expects us to use wisely what He has entrusted to us; He expects us to invest it. He expects us to put it to work and make it grow, not bury it.

The bottom line of this parable is found in Matthew 25:29, and we ought to plant it firmly in our minds. Those who manage well what they have been given are going to be given more and will have an abundance. Keep in mind that God's wealth is not limited to material things. God's idea of prosperity includes material things but is not limited to them. God's wealth also includes our salvation, our health, our family, our friends, our love, joy, peace, contentment, and other things that we cannot buy with money.

Tips on Finding Abundance

When your outgo exceeds your income, you have three options to solve your problem. Even when you have a balanced budget and you are not having a budget problem, these three areas can help you have greater joy and peace and help you find an even greater abundance in your budget.

Look at it any way you desire—to solve a problem or to find a greater abundance—here are your three option areas:

- Find options to increase your present income.
- Find options to lower existing outgo.
- Find options to control your future spending.

Pray for God to reveal options to you. Make

a list of the options He reveals to you. List every possible solution—not just the ones that sound the easiest or most appealing. List them even if you don't want to do them or will never do them. If it is something that you or anyone in your shoes could do, then list it. God may not reveal every option to you the first day, so keep praying daily for Him to keep on revealing options for you to add to your list.

As you listen for options, list them, pray over them for peace, and then act on them and record your responses. You will have visible evidence of how God is directing you and blessing your obedience to His way of managing money. This system is simply a tangible way to record your testimony day by day of how God loves you and is blessing you so that you can "enjoy an even greater abundance."

The following is a starter list of possible options to increase your income:

- The provider could find a second job.
- The provider could work overtime on his or her present job.
- The provider could find odd jobs as available.

- The provider could prepare for a higher-paying job with the same employer.
- The provider could seek a different, higher-paying primary job.
- The spouse, where applicable, could start employment.
- The spouse, where applicable, if already employed, could do the first five items above.
- Older children in the family could take part-time jobs to help the family budget.
- You could sell any assets or items you no longer need.
- You could have a garage or yard sale.
- You could turn a hobby into an income producer.
- You could rent some of your appropriate assets to others.
- You could share your need with a relative who may bless you with a gift.

The following is a starter list of possible options to reduce your outgo:

- Sell any asset not needed and pay off the debt remaining on that asset.

- Share your housing (rent part) to lower your outgo for the rent or mortgage.
- Prepay part or all of your debts from savings or other assets.
- Ask each creditor to lower your interest rate and monthly payment, if possible, even if it is only for a temporary period. Do not be bashful about asking creditors for help; you may be surprised what they offer.
- Reorganize your debts to extend the repayment time and lower your average interest rate and monthly payment.
  - Loan consolidation
  - Equity loan
  - Refinancing of home
- Increase your income and prepay your debts.
- Cut back on your spending and prepay your debts.
- Look for a bank that has low or no service charges for their accounts.

A NOTE ABOUT CONSOLIDATING DEBT

There are some dangers in reorganizing your debts. Seventy-five percent of those who reorganize their debts with any type of a loan consolidation find themselves right back to the same high payment in only twelve months. Why? First, because they did not overcome ignorance with wisdom and learn how to manage well. Second, because they did not change their attitude about spending, borrowing, using credit cards, or living within their income. Many times those 75 percent who end up right back where they were with high monthly payments have the wrong attitude: "Now that we have our loan consolidation with lower payments, we can take that luxury vacation or buy that newer car or that big-screen television." When they do such things, the outgo for debt payment goes right back up. The loan consolidation did not solve their problem; it only treated the symptom for twelve months. More money does not solve our problem if we continue to mismanage when we get more money.

I encourage you to fix your level of spending below your income level, especially if you consolidate your debts to reduce your outgo. Try to operate on a cash basis from this point on, especially if you consolidated your loans, to prevent your outgo from creeping up above your income again.

The following is a starter list of possible options to control your future spending:

- Shop with a need list for food.
- Use coupons only for items on your need list.
- Do not use coupons until you make a price comparison with other brands, especially generic or store brands.
- Shop for price, not labels, in one or more stores.
- When shopping for food, compare fresh, frozen, and canned to determine the best price per serving.
- Shop with a need list for clothing and all other items.
- Avoid carrying or using credit cards for anything.
- Combine errands into a maximum of one trip per week.
- Carry lunch to work and school.
- Eliminate junk food.
- Order only water to drink when eating out.
- Cut back a little in all budget categories.
- Reduce the miles you drive through better planning.
- Reduce the times you turn on electric lights and appliances.

- Use electric fans to allow warmer air-conditioning settings to reduce electric bills.
- Open windows and shut off air-conditioning or heat as weather permits.
- Stay out of stores unless you have an item on your need list.
- Make all future purchases in cash, or pay for higher-priced items by check.
- Do not let your mortgage lender retain overages in escrow accounts; ask for refunds.

We are creatures of habit, and habits are easily formed but hard to break. An extra effort needs to be made to change our poor habits into better habits. Most of our spending is simply a result of our habits—our habitual ways of buying clothes, food, household items, and gifts for example. Do we look in the pantry, closet, or garage, make a list of our needs, and buy only those items on our needs list? Do we make a list of errands to do and then plan the best time and most direct route to save both gasoline and time? Most errands could be planned for one day a week or every two weeks on the way to or from work. If we make a grocery list and shop weekly, we should not run out of needed food items and end up going to the grocery store three to four times a week. What are your spending habits? Could they be improved?

To be successful in cutting back on all future spending requires the committed faithful support and cooperation of every member in the family. God will bless harmony in the home. Relationships are more important than money, so be sure you do what you do in love. Love is the greatest motivator in the world. More important than what we are doing in our planning and spending is why we are doing it. Our purpose for doing anything should be to bring glory to God, to serve others, and to provide for our needs.

4.

Understand Your Assets: Calculating Your Gross Monthly Income

God told us in Proverbs 18:13 (TLB), "What a shame—yes, how stupid!—to decide before knowing the facts!" The purpose of Form 1 (see page 153) is to gather facts from the past calendar year so that you can have a base on which to project your future budget. Completing Form 1 is most important, even if your past circumstances or income is not the same as your future circumstances or income.

Instructions

- Use pencil.
- Use any records available to arrive at the most accurate figures.
- Round all figures off to the nearest dollar (e.g., $941.36 should be written as $941).
- Convert all figures to monthly amounts. For example, $100/week x 52 weeks/year = $5,200/year ÷ 12 months = $433/month.
- Fill in every blank.

- If you do not have an income or expense (outgo) in any item, simply insert a dash (—). If self-employed, do not include business income or expenses on this form; use only the net profit and wages received from your business that were brought home for family as your family gross income.

- Include all income from any source, and include all expenses for any reason. Do not list any item in more than one place, but include every dollar somewhere. If you can't find a listing on Form 1 for one of your sources of income or outgo, then write in the item under the Other category.

- Remember to write in the average monthly income and outgo for each item (e.g., for the electric bill average, add up all the electric bills you paid in the past calendar year and divide that total by 12 months to determine the accurate monthly average). If you pay for most items by check and you have your checks returned by the bank, simply make a separate pile of checks for each category—telephone, water, food, clothing—then total each pile and divide by 12.

- This exercise will not include the items that you paid for in cash, so you need to estimate all cash expenditures. If you do not have a record for an item, such as eating out, estimate the amount per week (as expenditures can more accurately be recalled in weekly time periods); then convert it to a monthly figure as shown above.

- Do not go back and change any figures except to correct errors or oversights. Do not try to balance the income with the expenses by changing figures. Simply record all items as accurately as possible and let the difference remain as it is. The smaller the difference is, the better record keeper you are.

Calculating Incoming Funds

For all salaried persons, we do not use take-home pay, only gross income. Payroll deductions, such as insurance, credit union savings, debt payments, bonds, union dues, and so forth, should be listed in the appropriate expense category, described later in this chapter. List all gross income per month. Gross income is the amount earned before any deductions, such as taxes, Social Security, hospitalization premiums, and the like are made. Be sure to include commissions, bonuses, fees, tips, pensions, and Social Security received. Also include other income, such as gifts, inheritance, child support, alimony, and loans. Other income should include money received from the sale of cars, boats, and other items.

Investment income should be listed only as net profit or loss (a loss of $120 per month should be listed as a minus: –$120). For multiple investments, combine the results.

Self-employment income should be listed only as a net profit or loss. For a sole proprietor, not incorporated, this would be the net from business that was taken home to provide for the family before paying income taxes.

People who receive pensions or have Social Security incomes should list their gross income before anything is taken out, such as IRS withholding or Medicare premiums. IRS withholdings should be listed under Outgo Per Month, category 2: Taxes. Medicare premiums deducted from your check should be listed under category 6: Insurance. After listing all income, add it up and place the total amount in the space to the

right of the boldface words GROSS INCOME PER
MONTH.

Calculating Outgoing Funds

Use the best records you have to determine the
most accurate figures possible. If you keep written records, use them. Some information could
be obtained from receipts. Another way—possibly
the most accurate way—to determine your outgo
over a twelve-month period, is to take all the
checks written in that period and divide them
up into separate piles—all electric bills in one
pile, all telephone bills in another, etc. When all
checks for the twelve-month period are divided,
total each pile and divide by 12 to get your average per month. Then record the monthly average
on Form 1 in the corresponding category item.

Category 1: Tithe and Offerings

The total amount in the Tithe and Offerings category should include all monetary gifts and donations to churches and religious organizations,
whether given by check or cash. Do not include
noncash donations, as we are dealing with cash
flow in budgeting, not tax deductions. All charitable contributions should be listed under the

Miscellaneous category of Gifts. Remember to convert your weekly church contributions to a monthly amount. For example, $100/week x 52 ÷ 12 months/year = $433/month. Do not take $100/week x 4, as that will account for only 48 weeks, not 52 weeks in a year.

Category 2: Taxes

The total amount in the Tax category should include all amounts paid out in the past twelve-month period. This total would include Federal Income Tax, Social Security, and Medicare amounts withheld or paid, also state, county, or municipal income tax withheld or paid, if applicable. This category does not include sales tax, real estate taxes, or other types of taxes. These non-withholding taxes are listed elsewhere on the form. An easy way to determine this information is to obtain the withholding taxes from your most recent W-2 forms or your income tax return and add to that amount any other amounts that may have been paid directly to the IRS in that same calendar year. Then divide the total paid by 12 to get your monthly average.

After completing your total gross income, subtract category totals 1 and 2 from the total gross income and record the balance as NET SPENDABLE INCOME.

Category 3: Housing

If you are renting, cross out the word *Mortgage*. If you are buying, cross out the word *Rent*. If you have more than one mortgage, list the second mortgage under Other. If your mortgage payment includes *principle*, *interest*, *taxes*, and *insurance*, bracket those words and draw a line to the total payment. If your mortgage payment includes only principle and interest, list your insurance and real estate taxes in the spaces provided. Remember to include special tax assessments and flood insurance if applicable. Add up your past 12 electric bills and divide by 12 to get your average electric expense per month; do the same for gas, water, trash removal, and telephone.

Your average monthly maintenance includes such items for the house as painting, electric and plumbing repairs, carpet cleaning, bug spraying, lawn care, fertilizer, etc. The Other category includes home improvements and purchases of furniture, appliances, and the like. If furniture and appliances are financed, they should be included under Debts (category 7), not housing.

In summary, this category should include all money necessary to pay for and operate the home.

Category 4: Food

The Food category includes all purchases made at the grocery store, including nonfood items and pet food. Also include food items purchased elsewhere, such as at fruit stands and convenience stores, and ready-to-eat foods that are brought home to eat. Do not include eating out or food purchased for lunch at work or school. Eating out while at work or school goes under Miscellaneous, category 13, and eating out for entertainment goes under Entertainment and Recreation, category 8. If you did not keep records, then estimate the amount spent per week and convert that amount to a monthly figure.

Category 5: Transportation

If you have payments on two cars, add another space and list them separately. If you changed cars during the year, add up the total amount paid on each car and divide the annual total by 12 to obtain the average monthly payment. List the total spent monthly for gas for all cars under Gas. Compute the total spent for insurance on all cars for the year and divide by 12 months to obtain the average monthly insurance expense. Remember to convert the annual license tag expense to a monthly figure. Auto Maintenance and Repair should include such things as grease, oil changes, tires, batteries, and tune-ups. The Replacement item is to be used only if you replaced or purchased a vehicle in the year for which you are recording this information (the past twelve-month calendar year). Use the amount of cash you paid out, not the sale price of the car, and divide by 12 to get the monthly average.

Category 6: Insurance

The Insurance category includes health, life, and disability insurance, but not home or auto insurance. Remember to include any premiums that are deducted from your paycheck. Include Medicare premiums that are deducted from your Social Security check in this category. Also include any health-care premiums that may be deducted from your pension check.

Category 7: Debts

The Debts category includes all monthly payments you paid in the twelve-month period to meet debts, such as credit cards, personal loans, medical debts, installment loans, and so on. Do not include home mortgages and automobile payments. If you pay your credit card balance in full each month when received, it is not included in this category but should be included in the category appropriate for the items purchased. If you buy gasoline for your auto with a credit card and pay the balance in full every month, the amount paid should be listed under the Auto category for gas. Remember: never list any one expenditure under two categories. Every dollar that comes in can only go out one time.

Category 8: Entertainment and Recreation

The Dining Out item is for entertainment only and does not include eating out while at work or school. Since most people do not keep records of the amounts spent eating out, including tips, we suggest that you estimate the average amount spent per week and convert that amount to a monthly figure: ($___ /week x 52 ÷ 12 = $___ /month). This category also includes trips and vacations as separate items. Trips includes all trips other than vacation. The type of expenses to include in both Trips and Vacations are such things as travel, lodging, food, entertainment, souvenirs, etc. Babysitting does not include child care while a parent works. Child care while a parent works should be listed under Miscellaneous Other as a write-in. Activities includes such things as movies, concerts, club dues, attendance or participation in sports events, and hobby expense. The Other item should be used as a write-in for recreational vehicles, sports equipment, boats, video rentals, and so on.

Category 9: Clothing

List your clothing expense for the year and divide by 12 to get your monthly average. Only include the clothing paid for in cash or charged on a credit card that was paid in full when the first bill for that item was received. All clothing bought on credit that was paid for on the credit installment plan should be listed under Debts, category 7. Shoes and clothing accessories should be included in this category.

Category 10: Savings

The amount you saved in the past year divided by 12 is your average amount saved monthly. The amount you saved should include the interest or dividend earned. Do not include any money you saved in the past year if you withdrew it during the past twelve months. One way to determine your average monthly savings is to write down your beginning savings balance as of the first day of the twelve-month period and then write down your savings balance at the end of the twelve-month period and subtract the difference. The difference divided by 12 is your average monthly increase or decrease. If you experienced a decrease because you drew out more than you added, list it as a negative (–) amount, (–$1,200/year ÷12 = –$100/month). If you have a negative amount, remember to subtract it from your total outgo. Do not add it by mistake.

Category 11: Investments

Savings are usually short-term undesignated funds saved; investments are long-term designated funds, such as IRAs, pensions, profit sharing, mutual funds, annuities, stocks, bonds, and real estate. Many people with low incomes may not have any amount in this category. Use the same method as used in Savings to determine your investment increase or decrease for the twelve-month period.

Category 12: Medical Expenses

The Medical Expenses category should include only those medical expenses that you paid out in the past twelve months that were not reimbursed by Medicare or your health insurance provider. Do not include your premium for medical insurance, as it was included under Insurance, category 6. Be sure to include such items as doctor and dentist bills, eye care and glasses, prescription medicine, hospital bills, ambulance, X-rays, and laboratory work. Do not include nonprescription medicine in this category. List it where you bought it—for example, grocery store or drugstore.

Category 13: Miscellaneous

This category includes expenses that do not fit anywhere else. List all drugstore purchases except prescription medicine, which should be listed in category 12. Drugstore Items should be all drugstore-type products and all drugstore-type stores. If you sometimes buy food at a drugstore, just leave it under Drugstore. If you buy cosmetics or other drugstore-type items from direct sales companies, you should include them under Drugstore Items.

Allowances for children and lunches at school for children or at work for parents should be included.

Subscriptions for newspapers, magazines, record clubs, and book clubs should be included.

Gifts, including gifts for birthdays, weddings, Christmas and other holidays, cards, stamps, and gifts to charitable organizations should be included.

Education includes courses for adults or children in private schools and colleges, and it includes all expenses including tuition, books, fees, transportation, and uniforms.

Pocket money is the money you put in your pocket at the beginning of the week and is gone at the end of the week. It is spent on miscellaneous items, such as snacks, drinks, mints, parking meters, bridge tolls, and other items not in any other category. Estimate a weekly amount; then convert it to monthly.

Pet store purchases and veterinarian charges should be included here. If your pet food was purchased at the grocery store or drugstore, just leave it in that category.

The Other category includes any item not included elsewhere that you are listing separately as a write-in. Such items may include child care while a parent works, child support paid out, alimony paid, attorney's fees, accounting fees, bank service charges, union dues, loans to others, and so on.

Calculating Final Totals

Now add the totals of categories 3 through 13 and place the total as TOTAL EXPENSES. Then bring the same total to line B, the LESS EXPENSE line, and subtract it from line A, the NET SPENDABLE INCOME. The answer should be placed on line C, the DIFFERENCE line. If the answer is a negative answer—the expenses were greater than the net spendable income—place a minus sign (–) in front of the answer.

Do not go back and change any figures to try to make your net spendable income balance with your total expenses. Only make changes for greater accuracy if you discovered an error in your previous figures. You need to be honest with yourself, so do not make up any amounts to balance your income or outgo.

This form will reveal to you the accuracy of your record keeping and identify where your income came from and where it went. It is simply a one-page history of your past year's family financial activity put into budget form.

Form 1 has two columns. At this time fill in only the PAST calendar year figures in the first column on the single lines on a blank form in the back of the book. Do not write in the boxes marked PROJECTED at this time. This step will be addressed in Chapter 6.

5.

Recognize Your Responsibilities: Keeping Track of Debt

The purpose of Form 2 (page 154) is to make visible the nature of your debts, the amount unpaid, the amount past due, the monthly obligations, and the cost to borrow. If any debts are seriously past due, they deserve immediate attention and should be given top priority. If you are past due on any debts, it is a good idea to contact creditors by phone and in writing also, and let them know you are working on a plan to bring their account current as soon as possible. It is not a good idea to make promises to pay amounts by certain dates if you cannot keep your promise. This form will help you organize and analyze all debts as of the day you prepare the list. A "debt" is money you owe that could be paid in full and the debt would not continue or reoccur without action on your part. Rent, utility bills, insurance premiums, etc. are not debts—they are operating expenses.

God tells us in Romans 13:8 (KJV), "Owe no man any thing." The only way we can owe no man anything is to get out of debt and stay out of debt.

When you complete Form 2, your debts will be organized so you can analyze options to get out of debt.

Instructions

- Use pencil.
- Round all figures off to the nearest dollar ($941.36 should be written as $941).
- Divide debts into one of three categories: (1) Housing (your primary house only), (2) Auto (transportation), (3) All other debts.

Column 1: To Whom Owed

List the name of the bank, finance company, merchant, doctor, hospital, credit card company, or other creditor from whom you borrowed the money. If it is a relative or friend, list that person's name. Under All Other Debts, list any remaining debts from the largest unpaid balance down to the smallest unpaid balance.

Column 2: Used for What

Under Housing, list first mortgage, second mortgage, equity line loan, home improvement loan, or a more specific identification, such as room addition or swimming pool.

Under Auto, list the year and make of the car, truck, motorcycle, or other vehicle you use as transportation. If the auto is leased, place the word *leased* in the Interest column.

Under All Other Debts, list what the money was used for: furniture; appliances; equipment loans; credit cards; student loans; loan consolidations; personal loans from friends, family, employer, bank, finance companies; all medical debts to doctors, hospitals, laboratories, etc. List all other types of installment debts.

Column 3: Current Unpaid Balance

List the current unpaid balance as of the date you are completing the form. As instructed in column 1, the debts listed in the All Other Debts category should start with the largest balance down to the smallest balance. If the vehicle is leased, list the balance as the number of payments remaining multiplied by the monthly lease amount.

Column 4: Past Due Amount

List the dollar amount that is past due as of the date the form is prepared. If the date of the form is the 12th and you had a payment due on the

10th and it was not paid, it is past due and should be listed in the Past Due column—even if you have a ten-day grace period. It is still two days past the due date. If you do not have an amount past due, place a dash (—) in this column.

Column 5: Monthly Payment

List the contract monthly payment only. Do not list the amount you paid if it was more or less than the contract amount. If you do not have a monthly payment, place a dash (—) in this column.

Column 6: Interest Rate

If your current statement does not have the interest rate annual percentage rate (APR), obtain it from your original note, security agreement, or contract. If your interest rate is adjustable, note near the percent "ADJ" so you know it may change. If adjustable, list the current rate as of the date the form is prepared. If you do not have an interest charge, place a dash (—) in this column. No interest rate is stated on lease payments; however, you can be sure interest is included in the contract.

Debt Examples Not to List

- Rent is not a debt. You can't pay it off.

- Current utility bills are not considered a debt.
- Mortgages on investments do not get listed on Form 2, as this form is for family debt only.
- Vehicles used exclusively for business should not be listed on Form 2.
- Do not list any debts for a self-employed business, full-time or part-time, on Form 2. A self-employed business includes any endeavor where you work and receive income other than salary, bonus, and tips. You have your own business or you are classified as an independent contractor working for others.

When All Debts Are Listed

Add columns 3, 4, and 5 in each category and place the totals on the total lines in the spaces with the bold-lined boxes. If you have debts in all three categories, you should have three separate totals, one for each of the three categories.

After you have developed your new budget, this form will be used to analyze options to get out of debt and stay out of debt. Do not try to do this until you have your new budget completed.

6.

Know Your Limits: Creating and Maintaining a Balanced Budget

Utilizing Form 3

The purpose of Form 3 (page 155) is to determine what the average family with your level of income is spending in the various categories. Later in the chapter we will discus Form 4 (page 156), which will help you evaluate your past monthly budget and compare it to your recommended monthly budget to create a new projected monthly budget.

Step 1: Determine Your Projected Gross Annual Income

If your projected annual income is going to be very close to your past annual income, you can use the same gross monthly income as recorded on your Form 1 (times 12 to get your gross annual income). Most individuals and families will have a different income each year due to job changes, salary increases, changed hours, bonuses, commissions, and other factors.

The purpose of this step is to estimate as

accurately as possible your realistic projected income. It is better to estimate your income on the lower side so you don't set your budget spending too high. When estimating your projected income, use Form 1 as your worksheet and write in your projections for each source of income in the boxes to the right of each source.

After projecting your gross average monthly income from all sources for the next twelve months on Form 1, transfer that total gross average monthly income to the box on Form 3, line A.

Multiply line A by 12 to determine your gross annual income. Now stop working on Form 3 and complete Step 2.

Step 2: Select Your Percentage Guide

Refer to the Percentage Guide chart on the following page for various levels of income. Select the income level that is the closest to your projected gross annual income from Form 3, line B. Mark an X on the Percentage Guide above the level you selected. Then transfer all percentages in your income level from the guide to Form 3, column 2. For incomes less than $25,000, use the $25,000-level percentages. For incomes over

PERCENTAGE GUIDE FOR FAMILY INCOME

FAMILY OF FOUR

(The Net Spendable percentages also are applicable to "Head of Household" families of three)

GROSS HOUSEHOLD INCOME	$25,000 or less	$35,000	$45,000	$55,000	$65,000	$85,000	$115,000
1. Tithe	10%	10%	10%	10%	10%	10%	10%
2. *Tax - Married/Head of Household	10%	12%	15%	16%	17%	21%	23%
*Tax - Single/No Dependents	17%	18%	22%	24%	26%	28%	29%
NET SPENDABLE INCOME - Married/HOH	$20,000	$27,300	$33,750	$40,700	$47,450	$58,650	$77,050
Single	$18,250	$25,200	$30,600	$36,300	$41,600	$52,700	$70,150
3. Housing	38%	36%	32%	30%	30%	30%	29%
4. Food	14%	12%	13%	12%	11%	11%	11%
5. Auto	14%	12%	13%	14%	14%	13%	13%
6. Insurance	5%	5%	5%	5%	5%	5%	5%
7. Debts	5%	5%	5%	5%	5%	5%	5%
8. Entertainment	4%	6%	6%	7%	7%	7%	8%
9. Clothing	5%	5%	5%	6%	6%	7%	7%
10. Savings	5%	5%	5%	5%	5%	5%	5%
11. Investment	-----	5%	5%	5%	5%	5%	5%
12. Medical	5%	4%	4%	4%	4%	4%	4%
13. Miscellaneous	5%	5%	7%	7%	8%	8%	8%

CHART 1

* For all self-employed persons add 7.65% of Gross Income for Self-Employment Tax

$115,000, use the $115,000-level percentages. If your income is exactly in the middle of two levels, use the level above or below—the one you think may be more correct if circumstances change for any reason. Do not change any percentages in the guide except for singles without dependents in category 2, Taxes. Singles without dependents use the percentages on the singles line for their Tax Guide. All others use the category 2 tax percentage on the Married/Head of Household line. Do not omit a category just because you don't have any money spent in that category. If you do not have any money spent on Debts (category 7), do not omit the percent for that category nor transfer that percent to another category.

This is only a guide for families with your income level. It is not your budget, not your limit, but simply a guide to help you identify any of your excess spending or underspending as compared with the average family. You will note that the $25,000-level income does not have any percentage for Investment (category 11). That is because the average family with that income level is not investing; usually it takes all their income to provide for their present needs. This does not mean that families in that income level could not or should not allocate funds for investments.

You will also note that category 1, Tithe (God), is 10 percent for all levels of income. While all other percentages are based on the average family, the average family is not giving God 10 percent of their gross income. So we use the Bible, God's book of finance, to obtain our 10 percent minimum percentage guide.

These percentages are based on the average family of four persons. Do not change any percentages on the guide just because you are a family of one or twelve. Your adjustments will be made on Form 4, column 5, which is your budget analysis, where you will later record your budget.

The percentage in categories 1 and 2, Tithe and Taxes, are based on gross income from all sources. The percentage in categories 3 through 13 total 100 percent of the Net Spendable amount.

Step 3: Determine the Guideline Amounts for Your Income Level

After you have transferred all the percentages from your income level column of the Percentage Guide chart to your Form 3, column 2, calculate the guideline dollar amounts for your gross income. Insert your gross monthly income from line A of Form 4 to column 3, categories 1 and 2, as that is your multiplier for those two categories only. Next, multiply the Tithe (God) percent in column 2 by your multiplier in column 3, and place the answer in column 4 on the same line. Remember to round off all figures to the nearest dollar. Then complete category 2, Taxes (Government), in the same manner. When both categories 1 and 2 are complete, add them up and place the total on line C, column 4.

Next, subtract line C from line A (GROSS MONTHLY INCOME). The difference is your net spendable guideline income and is placed on line D in the box. Before you proceed, double-check your math up to this point, because this NET SPENDABLE amount is your multiplier for categories 3 through 13, and if it is wrong, all the remaining answers will be wrong. To proof your work, recalculate all your figures, add line D and line C, and your answer should be line A.

Now use line D (NET SPENDABLE INCOME) as your multiplier for categories 3 through 13, and insert that amount in column 3 for each of the remaining categories. Next, multiply the percentage in column 2, category 3 (Housing), by the multiplier, column 3 (NET SPENDABLE INCOME), and record your answer on the same line in column 4. Remember to round off all your answers to the nearest dollar in column 4.

Now complete categories 4 through 13 in the same manner. When all categories are completed, add column 4, categories 3 through 13, and place your answer on line E in the box.

Line E, NET SPENDABLE TOTAL, should be the same as line D, NET SPENDABLE INCOME. If they are not the same but they are $1, $2, or $3 over or under, it is probably due to the rounding-off process. If that is the case, you need to force a balance. If line E is $2 over your line D, then subtract $1 from any two categories from 3 through 13 to force line E to equal line D. If line E is $1 under your line D, then add $1 to any of the categories 3 through 13 to force line E to equal line D. If your line E is $4 or more over or under, you probably made an error in your multiplication or in recording the correct percentage in column 2. A double check of percentages can be made from the percentage guide. If you add the percentages in column 2, categories 3 through 13, they should equal 100 percent. You are now ready to proceed to your budget analysis, Form 4 (page 156).

Utilizing Form 4

The purpose of Form 4 is to analyze how your past budget compares with the guide for your level of income in each category so you can identify the problem areas. You cannot solve any problem until you identify it. Column 3 of Form 4 helps you identify your problem categories for your level of income.

After you analyze your problem categories, you then have the facts to plan a better-balanced budget for the future months and years.

Step 1: List Your Past Budget Totals

Transfer all your totals from Form 1 (Past Monthly Budget recorded on the lines) to Form 4, column 1.

Step 2: List Your Projected Budget Guide

Transfer all your totals from Form 3 (Monthly Budget Guide, column 4 and lines A, D, and E) to Form 4, column 2.

Step 3: List the Differences

Subtract column 2 from column 1 in each category and record the difference in column 3. If column 2 is less than column 1, the difference in column 3 will be a positive (+), and if column 2 is greater than column 1, the difference in column 3 will be a negative (–). A plus sign (+) will indicate that your past spending or allocation for that category is greater than the guide. A minus sign (–) will indicate that your past spending or allocation for that category is less than the guide.

A plus sign usually means bad news, categories where you are spending or allocating too much. However, if you have a negative in categories 1, 10, or 11, that is bad news, indicating that you are undergiving to God, undersaving, or underinvesting for your level of income.

Step 4: Identify Your Largest to Smallest Differences

Disregard the plus and minus signs in column 3 and number the differences in column 4, rating from the largest difference (1) to the smallest difference (13). If you have two categories with the same difference (e.g., $91) and your next number to list is 5, number the first $91 as 5 and the second $91 as 6.

Column 4 will identify the categories with the biggest differences, either over or under, so you can start your corrections in those categories with the biggest differences first.

Usually the four biggest problem categories are

- Category 3, Housing (usually overspending)
- Category 5, Auto (usually overspending)
- Category 7, Debts (usually overspending)
- Category 10, Savings (unable to save because of overspending)

We overspend and overborrow for housing; we overspend and overborrow for autos; and we overspend and overborrow for all other items that are financed or bought on credit cards. Then we are not able to save, so we undersave for our income. Categories 3, 5, and 7 are directly debt related, and category 10 is indirectly debt related. Excessive debt prevents us from being able to save.

God tells us in Proverbs 21:20 (TLB), "The wise man saves for the future, but the foolish man spends whatever he gets." He is telling us to spend less and save more. Overspending for one's level of income is one of the greatest budget problems.

Step 5. Identify Your Problem Areas

Analyze every category on Form 4. Identify your problem areas, consider all the options you have to improve the balance between your income and outgo, and take action to be a better manager of what God has entrusted to you.

Do not complete Form 4, column 5 at this time. The following steps and guidelines will help you develop your new, better, and balanced budget now that you have an indication of what your budget should be.

Developing a Budget That Works for You

Step 1: Make a List of Ways to Improve

Before completing column 5 of Form 4, read the money saving hints in Chapter 11 (pp. 119–143). Check off all the ideas you are going to try now, and estimate how much you will save per month. Place the amount you will save to the left of each idea. Do not check off the items that you are already doing. You only want to know how much you are going to save in the future. You can add your own ideas and indicate how much they will save you. This list is not complete, nor does it include every idea for every budget; it is only a list to stimulate your thoughts on ways to cut future costs.

Step 2: Start Your New Projected Monthly Budget

Go back to your Form 1 (Average Monthly Income and Outgo) and use it as a worksheet for your projected budget in the months ahead. All projected estimates should be placed in the second column, in the boxes. You should have completed the projections for future income on Form 1 before doing your Form 3. Now complete all the projection estimates for your future outgo. Use the insight obtained from the overspending items on Form 4 as you proceed with developing your budget in this chapter.

Step 3: Time for an Attitude Adjustment?

Before you begin, you need to remember that we don't have money problems—we have attitude problems about money matters. Our first attitude change should be "Can I/we improve?" You should ask this question as you analyze each item of your outgo. If your budget does not balance the first time after you have completed your future projections on Form 1, then it is time to adopt another attitude. Second Attitude Change: "Is this item a need, a want, or a desire?" If the item is not a need, you could cut back or cut out the item from your future budget. Again, ask yourself the question as you analyze each item. If the budget does not balance the second time you go through your complete outgo on Form 1, you get a third chance, just as in baseball.

You need to prayerfully adopt the attitude that asks, "Can I/we make do or do without?" Ask yourself this question as you analyze each item. Some of you will have balanced your budget the first time, others the second or third time. If you were serious about improving and cut back or cut out each of the three times and you still don't have a balanced budget, we will assume you did everything you could to reduce your future outgo by this method.

Step 4: Now It Is Time for Action

Now that our attitude is what God wants it to be, we can begin to prepare our new outgo for the future on Form 1 in the boxes provided. Remember to use pencil so you can revise as needed. Project your future allocations for each item in each category. Every box should have a figure in it unless you do not plan to allocate any money for that item in the future. Complete categories 1 through 13, except 7 (Debts), 10 (Savings), and 11 (Investments). The asterisk at the bottom of the form is your reminder to leave these three items for last, until you know how much is in your abundance. When you have completed all the boxes the first time (except 7, 10, and 11), subtract 1 and 2 (Tithes and Taxes) from your projected gross monthly income to determine your projected net spendable income. Now add up your projected outgo of items 3 through 13 (except 7, 10, and 11). Then subtract that total from your projected net spendable income. The balance is the abundance in your budget that you can allocate toward 7 (Debts) if you have any, and 10 (Savings), and 11 (Investments). The minimum amount needed for 7 (Debts) from your abundance can be obtained from your Form 3, column 5 (All Other Debts total). The next category to allocate from your abundance is 10 (Savings). Every person should have some amount to allocate for savings. As we have learned, "The wise man saves for the future, but the foolish man spends whatever he gets" (Proverbs 21:20 TLB). We don't want to go through all the work to establish a budget only to be "foolish." The third category to allocate from your abundance is 11 (Investments). Not everyone, especially those with low incomes, will be able to allocate an amount toward investments. I do not recommend that you allocate money for investments if you are heavy in debt with little or no savings. Sometimes the best investment is getting out of debt, especially if you are paying high interest rates on any loans or credit cards.

Proverbs 3:27–28 (TLB) tells us, "Don't withhold payment of your debts. Don't say 'some other time,' if you can pay now." God wants you to get out of debt and pay now if you can.

Step 5: Transfer Your New Projected Monthly Budget

When all boxes are complete on Form 1 for your projected budget (even if it is not balanced), transfer all your category totals to Form 4 (Budget Analysis), column 5. Now compare your Form 4, column 2 (Monthly Budget Guide), with column 5 (Projected Monthly Budget) to see how close you are to the guide. Next, compare your Form 4, column 1 (Past Monthly Budget) with column 5 (Projected Monthly Budget) to see how you improved over your old budget.

7.

Needs vs. Wants: Setting Goals and Adopting Healthy Spending Habits

It takes discipline and commitment to reach our goals and become champions, winning the race. Discipline is simply setting the rules. That is, we need to establish a plan (budget) and then make the commitment—a promise or vow—to follow the plan. Sports champions do not win without setting goals (making plans) and then applying the commitment to practice (stay on course) and follow the plan.

Step 1: Keep Good Records

Many people who think they have a budget do not—they are simply record keepers. Excellent record keeping is not a budget, but it is essential in preparing, maintaining, and controlling a budget. Proverbs 27:23 (kjv) tells us, "Be thou diligent to know the state of thy flocks, and look well to thy herds." Being diligent means paying attention to detail, knowing where you stand. We may not be shepherds, but the principle taught here is that we need to know what we have and keep abreast of where it is and how it is being managed. Be diligent—keep good records!

After you have completed Forms 1 through 4, you are now ready to develop your budget control system. It's important to keep track of your current spending and compare it to your Projected Budget figures from Form 4. If your present monthly total is greater than your Projected Budget total, you have overspent or overallocated for that month. When you have overspent, place a circle around the category where the difference is occurring. The circle around the difference denotes an *O* for overspent.

If your monthly total is less than your Projected Budget total, you have underspent or underallocated for that month. When you have underspent, place a line under the difference for the appropriate category. The line under the difference denotes underspending.

Circles around categories 1 (God), 10 (Savings), and 11 (Investments) indicate you overgave, oversaved, or overinvested. Lines under categories 1, 10, and 11 indicate you undergave, undersaved, or underinvested. These three categories are not considered spending categories.

If you are married, both spouses should be aware of all budget matters, but only one at a time should be the record keeper. Why? Because, as the saying goes "Everybody's job is nobody's job." The wife says, "I thought you were going to pay the bill." The husband says, "I thought you were going to pay the bill." The result: no one paid the bill.

Accountability is the key to good record keeping. If one spouse agrees to be the record keeper, then the other spouse must be the reporter and report all income and outgo. This should be done in writing to avoid errors and misunderstandings. If each is accountable for a specific function and each performs that function daily, peace will result, records will be accurate, and God will be pleased. Having peace in the family about money matters is one of the best insurance policies you can obtain for a long, happy, successful marriage.

Step 2: Analyze Your Income and Outgo Monthly

Everything you have done up to this point has been gathering facts and organizing them so you can prudently analyze them and establish a lifestyle and budget plan that brings glory to God and meets your needs. Your next step is to analyze each category at the end of every month to determine how your monthly total compares with your projected budget.

If you have overspent in any category, you could then look back over the past month to see day by day if you could have done better. If so, you can double your efforts to improve next month in that category. Your overspending could be because you planned to cut back or do without an item, but you kept right on spending and disregarded your plan. If that is your analysis, you need to recommit to follow the plan next month.

If your overspending continues in the same category for three more months and you have done everything possible to follow your cutback plan, then you may have cut back that category's projected budget unrealistically. If that is the case, you may need to increase your budget for that category by decreasing the budget amount in another category.

If you have underspent in any category, you should analyze why. You may have underspent in the auto category for the month because you had no auto repairs and it was not the month to pay for the six-month auto insurance premium. This type of analysis needs no correction or adjustment.

If you undergave to God or undersaved, you should analyze why and correct it by overgiving or oversaving next month. It may take more than one month to correct it.

The importance of keeping good records will be seen as you analyze each category each month. When you keep good, accurate records by recording all income and outgo daily, it makes your monthly analysis clear and easy.

Step 3: Adjust Your Budget When Circumstances Change

Coming up with the perfect projected budget with your first effort is unlikely. You should do the best you can and then keep accurate records of income and outgo for at least three months before considering any modifications to your budget.

If you are overspending in the food category, or any category, for all three months, it could be because you are not following your plan to cut back your spending on food, or it could be because you unrealistically underbudgeted your allocation for food.

When you have an unrealistic amount

allocated in any category, you need to look at all other categories to see if you can cut back somewhere and increase the unrealistic amount. Your increases need to be offset by decreases totaling the same amount. Only modify those categories that have large differences that cannot wait for your six-month analysis.

We suggest that you analyze the first year of your projected budget quarterly for possible modifications, but make changes only when necessary. If your income changes substantially during the year, either up or down, you may need to modify your budget immediately.

Determining Real Need vs. Want

Too little income is not the problem; overspending for one's income level is where most people find themselves. One way to correct this matter is to determine our real need before we spend. Our basic needs are food, shelter, and clothing. Above those essentials, we need to honor God, pay our taxes, and secure transportation so that we can provide income. A budget helps us get all these needs organized. Good health and a good mind enable us to earn the money to meet the needs.

After honoring the Lord and paying our taxes,

we now have what we call discretionary spending to provide necessary items—food, shelter, clothing, and transportation. We need to analyze and prioritize our needs, wants, and desires. *Needs* are food, shelter, clothing, and for some people, transportation. *Wants* are food, shelter, clothing, and transportation of a greater quantity or a better quality. We may want more or better clothes, more or better quality food, or a better quality house or car. *Desires* are conveniences, luxuries, and extravagances—things that most of our grandparents got along without and we could get along without.

Now, there is nothing wrong with having our wants and desires if our budget permits it and God gives us a peace about having them. Our needs, wants, and desires are simply a priority list. Our first priority is to provide for the basic needs of our family. When those needs are met, we can move up to our wants—more and better quality. Then when we are able, we can move up to our desires. This priority list should keep us from buying a luxury car or boat when we can't afford to put food on the table.

When all income is allocated for a designated category, you must avoid spending for items not budgeted, or you will be living beyond your means, unless you modify your budget before buying. If you want to buy a $500 item that is not in your projected budget plan, you can see if there is any $500 allocation in the projected budget that has a lower priority than the $500 item you want to buy. If so, then you could substitute the unbudgeted $500 item for the lower-priority projected budget item. This is a way to avoid overspending and borrowing, which is more critical as the months and years go by. We urgently need to get out of debt and stay out of debt.

Another option to avoid overspending is to evaluate if the wanted $500 item has a higher priority than saving for the future. If so, we could withdraw from our existing savings and pay cash for the wanted item.

The bottom line is to be honest with yourself, establish your priorities, and buy your needs first, then wants, and only as you are able, your desires. Seek God's wisdom and direction for your decisions and your peace.

Keeping a Need List

To avoid overspending and impulse spending, prepare a list at home of things you need, after looking in your pantry, closet, and garage. If you don't need it after looking in these areas, you don't need it just because it has a sale tag on it in the store.

Starting a list at the beginning of each week and adding to it during the week may be helpful, but only go shopping once a week. If we shop by list only and limit our number of trips to the store, we will experience greater economy and spend less.

Use of Coupons

Many people clip coupons in an effort to save money. To really save money, you should use coupons only (1) if the item is already on your need list and (2) only after you have shopped for price. Do not make up your list from your coupons, or you will buy more than you need. Only use coupons after you made your need list from looking in the pantry, closet, and garage.

When comparing five-pound bags of rice, one popular brand was priced at $3.39 and offered a $.50 discount coupon. But the store brand was $1.79. The only difference was the price. The popular brand, even with the coupon, was $1.10 more than the store brand. We could throw away the popular brand coupon and save money. It is doubtful that the family at home who ate the rice could identify any difference.

Compare Price, Quality, and Service

Buying the lowest-priced item every time, especially household items and appliances, is not necessarily the wisest choice. We can buy a specific brand item from the store with the lowest price when the quality and service for the identical item are the same as another store. Also compare various sizes for the best price per ounce. Usually, but not always, the largest size is the best price per ounce. Another comparison is the number of servings per price. You could compare canned vegetables with frozen and fresh, for example, and determine the number of servings you can get from each. When we buy an item that needs to be serviced, we need to look at the probability of the store being in business when we need service and their reputation for reliable service and reasonable prices. Always look for a balance between price, quality, and service.

Use Cash and Avoid Buying on Credit

According to various surveys, you can save from 28 to 34 percent when you avoid credit and pay cash. Looking at it another way, you will spend 28 to 34 percent more if you buy with credit cards. Merchants will pay credit card companies 3 percent to 5 percent to permit you to use credit cards in their store because they know you are likely to spend more when you use credit. The credit card companies take approximately 5 percent as a loss in their collections, but on an average 18 percent interest charge, they still net 13 percent plus merchant fees.

If you save $28 on every $100 you spend, you will have more money to save, spend, or honor the Lord. This is just another way to find an abundance in your budget. Keep in mind that every dollar you pay in interest is money you are throwing out the window.

Discipline yourself to break down your paycheck into specific amounts of cash or amounts to deposit into various accounts. Stick to your plan and limit your spending to budgeted items. If your plan works on paper, it will work in reality. You should not decide to spend based on the cash in your pocket or the balance in your checkbook. Once you have a balanced budget, you should only spend based on the amount allocated in your projected budget, because all dollars coming in are already allocated to go out. If you do not follow your written plan, you will have wasted the time you took to develop it.

How to Balance Your Checkbook

Most of us have not taken a course in school on how to balance a checkbook, and people of all ages have told me they do not know how to do so. Those who balance their checkbooks use slightly different methods. The method is not as important as the result—a balanced checkbook.

The following is one method you could use if you get your checks back with your bank statement:

- Notice that your statement lists your checks in numerical order. If you get your checks back, verify that all the checks are yours and that you or an authorized person signed all the checks.
- Verify that all the deposits you made are listed on your statement.
- Verify that all debits (checks or other withdrawals) and credits on the statement are correct and entered in your check register or on your check stubs.

- Look at your last monthly statement to determine which checks were outstanding and did not clear in time for your last statement.
- Verify that all outstanding checks from last month cleared this month. If not, list them as outstanding again this month.
- Complete the reconciliation form on the back of your bank statement by entering the ending balance of your statement plus any deposits not credited on that statement. From that total, subtract the total of outstanding checks to get your balance. This balance should agree with your checkbook balance after entering in your checkbook all charges, deductions, and interest shown on that statement.

If your account does not balance, check the following:

- Have you entered the amount of each check in your checkbook accurately?
- Are all deposit amounts, including interest, entered in your checkbook as shown on the bank statement?

- Have all charges been deducted from your checkbook?
- Have you double-checked the additions and subtractions in your checkbook?
- Have you brought the correct balance forward from one checkbook page to another?
- Have all checks written and other withdrawals been deducted from your checkbook?

If you have done all the above and it still does not balance, it is time to seek help from a qualified person or from your bank. Yes, it is possible—it could be a bank error.

8.

Thinking Ahead: Buying Smart and Saving for the Future

Since God owns everything—including all our possessions—we have a responsibility and accountability to Him for the way we manage money while we pass through life. While God owns it all, He wants us to enjoy it. We find His ownership and His plan for us to enjoy it in 1 Corinthians 10:26 (TLB): "For the earth and every good thing in it belongs to the Lord and is yours to enjoy."

If we are not enjoying what God has provided, it is not His fault. We need to look in the mirror and ask God, "What do You want me to change so that I can enjoy what You have provided?" Something—our attitude, our priorities, or our actions—needs to change if we are not enjoying what God has provided.

The Importance of Saving

One of the most important priorities of money—after earning it honestly and honoring God with the first part—is to SAVE FOR THE FUTURE.

"The wise man saves for the future, but the foolish man spends whatever he gets" (Proverbs 21:20 TLB). The average family in the United States is spending 122 percent of its income and is NOT wise (saving for the future) and NOT foolish (spending whatever they get), but is MORE THAN FOOLISH (spending more than they receive).

Proverbs 21:5 (TLB) teaches us "Steady plodding brings prosperity; hasty speculation brings poverty." Starting early in life to regularly save little by little will lead you to financial prosperity. A good commonsense reason to save for the future is that we don't know what the future may bring.

In saving for the future, we should avoid get-rich-quick schemes, as Proverbs 28:22 (TLB) warns: "Trying to get rich quick is evil and leads to poverty."

There are a lot of good reasons to save, one of which can be found in 1 Timothy 5:8 (TLB): "Anyone who won't care for his own relatives when they need help, especially those living in his own family, has no right to say he is a Christian. Such a person is worse than the heathen." Jesus says in John 15:12 (TLB), "I demand that you love each other as much as I love you." Loving is not an option. He also tells us in John 13:34 (TLB), "I am giving a new commandment to you now—love each other just as much as I love you." He adds in the next verse "Your strong love for each other will prove to the world that you are my disciples" (v. 35 TLB). And three times Jesus says that the demonstration of our love for Him is our obedience: "If you love me, obey me" (John 14:15 TLB); "The one who obeys me is the one who loves me" (v. 21 TLB); and "Anyone who doesn't obey me doesn't love me" (v. 24 TLB).

God is saying, "Just do what I am asking you to do." What is God asking us to do? Well, He is asking us to understand, first of all, that He is the owner and that we are the managers. Our purpose is to bring glory to Him, to earn money honestly, to return to the Lord the first part of what we earn, to give the government its share, and to save some for the future so that we can provide for family and help others in need. Jesus said, "It is more blessed to give than to receive" (Acts 20:35 KJV). God wants to bless us, but when we mismanage and do not have anything to give, we rob ourselves of the blessing God intended us to have. If we don't obey God and provide for family, we don't love Him.

If we don't love our family, God's love is not in our hearts. So we have a responsibility to provide for family. No place in the Bible does it say that when we have a need we should go to the government or to the bank. It tells us that family should help family. That is God's way.

We need to fix our spending level in our budget plan below our level of income so that we can be obedient to God and save for the future. God also told us in Proverbs 6:6 (TLB), "Take a lesson from the ants, you lazy fellow. Learn from their ways and be wise!" What do ants do? When there is a surplus of food in the summertime, they store up for the uncertain future. And guess what? There is no king ant or queen ant giving instructions. Without being told, the ant is saving for the uncertain future. We should do the same.

On the next page is a chart that demonstrates how systematic saving started early can assure you a greater steady income for the rest of your life as you get older and may not be physically able to work.

SAVINGS GROWTH

Select the amount per month you want to save, then save that amount every month.
(All figures are based on 5 percent compounded daily)

SAVING FOR THE FUTURE

IF YOU SAVE:	FOR:	YOU WILL ACCUMULATE	YOU CAN WITHDRAW FOREVER
$ 20.00 / month	10 years	$ 3,120.00	$ 13.00 / month
	15 years	$ 5,373.00	$ 22.00 / month
	20 years	$ 8,265.00	$ 34.00 / month
	30 years	$ 16,746.00	$ 70.00 / month
	40 years	$ 30,729.00	$ 128.00 / month

$ 20.00/month is 5% of $400.00/month or $ 4,800/year

IF YOU SAVE:	FOR:	YOU WILL ACCUMULATE	YOU CAN WITHDRAW FOREVER
$ 50.00 / month	10 years	$ 7,801.00	$ 32.00 / month
	15 years	$ 13,432.00	$ 56.00 / month
	20 years	$ 20,662.00	$ 86.00 / month
	30 years	$ 41,865.00	$ 174.00 / month
	40 years	$ 76, 821.00	$ 319.00 / month

$ 50.00/month is 5% of $1,000.00/month or $ 12,000.00/year

IF YOU SAVE:	FOR:	YOU WILL ACCUMULATE	YOU CAN WITHDRAW FOREVER
$ 100.00 / month	10 years	$ 15,601.00	$ 65.00 / month
	15 years	$ 26,863.00	$ 112.00 / month
	20 years	$ 41,323.00	$ 172.00 / month
	30 years	$ 83,729.00	$ 348.00 / month
	40 years	$ 153,643.00	$ 639.00 / month

$ 100.00/month is 5% of $ 2,000.00/month or $24,000.00/year

CHART 2

Buying Smart

Impulse buying is one of the biggest wastes in our budget. We go to the store to buy two things and come home with ten. We just bought eight items on impulse. Some people say, "I just went to the store to browse," and they came home with three bags full of "browse." We all are guilty of impulse spending to some degree. How do we control impulse spending?

- Carry no credit cards.
- Carry no checks.
- Carry no extra cash.
- Carry only the cash needed to buy those items on your need list, which you prepared at home after looking in the pantry, closet, and garage.

These guidelines may seem rather severe, but they work. When we have no way to impulse spend, we won't spend impulsively. Most people want emergency money in their wallet or pocketbook. I agree that is wise. But I suggest that you select one bill—a $20, $50, or $100—as your emergency money and then place that bill in a hidden location in your wallet so you won't be tempted to spend it. Remember, that bill is emergency money only, and you don't have an emergency every day! That is, you don't spend it every day and then replace it with another bill when you get home. This system will work if you follow the plan.

Seek Counsel on Big-Ticket Items

None of us knows all that needs to be known about every item we buy, especially big-ticket items. Recall the proverbs we cited earlier: "What a shame—yes, how stupid!—to decide before knowing the facts!" (18:13 TLB) and "Without consultation, plans are frustrated, but with many counselors they succeed" (15:22 NASB). God wants us to get the facts by seeking counsel from more than one counselor, especially if it is the salesperson.

We have several ways to get the facts and seek counsel. Information on many items can be found in *Consumer Reports Buying Guide*, which is available at most public libraries. We can talk to more than one company representative or salesperson. Another way to get information is to talk to other people who previously bought the item.

How to Have Transportation without Monthly Payments

Many people today think that having a monthly payment on a car, truck, or van is a way of life. It is an expensive way to provide transportation. People who trade cars frequently, finance the new car before the old one is paid in full, and put very little down when they trade are in a situation we call upside-down financing. This usually means that at no time during the life of the loan can you sell your car for enough money to pay off the loan. The depreciation on your car makes the value of your car go down faster than the balance of the loan.

Overspending and overborrowing on vehicles is one of the four biggest problem areas in most peoples' budgets. How do we solve this problem?

We can start by only buying a vehicle we can pay for in cash. This may mean beginning with an older car and saving extra money to upgrade to a newer car as we are able. With this plan we could end up buying a new car with all cash in a few years if we establish a budget and follow our plan to save on a regular systematic basis.

Finance Plan

Thirty years ago I made a decision about buying a car with limited cash. I obtained the facts about buying a new car (1981) at the end of the year after the next year's (1982) models had come out. The car I looked at was considered one year old but was new because it had no mileage. The sales price was $9,000. If I paid $1,000 down and financed $8,000 for three years at 12 percent interest, the payment would have been $302 per month. The interest would have totaled $2,880, which means I would have paid $11,880 for that $9,000 car. If I wanted lower monthly payments, I could have obtained an $8,000 loan at 12 percent for four years with payments of $247 per month. The interest would have totaled $3,840, which means I would have paid $12,840 to acquire that $9,000 car.

Most people do not realize that the longer the loan, the more interest you pay, and the more you pay to acquire the auto. They are only interested in the lower monthly payment. Many autos today are financed over five, six, and seven years just to keep the monthly payments down so buyers can qualify to finance them. That does not mean they can afford the car or that it is good for their budget.

Cash Plan

Back to my facts. What would happen if I took the $1,000 down payment and bought the best car I could find for $1,000 cash? At that time I could have bought an eight-year-old car for $1,000 cash. Had I done that and then added $3 to the $247, four-year finance plan to total $250 and then started saving $250 per month for 12 months, I would have saved $3,000 cash in one year. Then if I chose to upgrade my transportation by trading or selling my eight-year-old car that would be nine years old, I probably could have gotten $500 for it, which means I would have had $3,500 cash in one year to pay for a newer car. And I probably could have bought a four-year-old car for $3,500.

If I continued to save $250 per month for the second year, I would have had another $3,000. If I decided to upgrade my car at the end of the second year, I probably could have gotten $2,500 for the $3,500 car I bought a year earlier. I would then have had $3,000 plus $2,500, or $5,500, to pay cash for possibly a three-year-old car.

Since the feeling of driving a car without monthly payments is great, I would have continued saving $250 per month for the third year and had another $3,000. If I decided to upgrade again at the end of the third year, I probably could have gotten $4,000 for the $5,500 car I bought one year earlier. I would now have $7,000 cash to buy possibly a two-year-old car. Now, when I compare this point of my cash plan with the purchase of the $9,000 new car on a three-year finance plan, I discover an interesting fact. After three years at $302 a month, that $9,000 car would finally be paid in full, but what would be its value? It would be $4,230—about half the new-car price. I could buy a car for half price if I had patience to wait and saved the cash in advance. Now compare that new car value three years later at $4,230 with the car I could have bought in three years on the cash plan for $7,000. On the finance plan, I could have had a $4,230 car in three years; on the cash plan, I could have had a $7,000 car in three years.

If I projected my cash plan to save $250 per month for the fourth year, I would have saved another $3,000. If I decided to upgrade again at the end of the fourth year, I probably could have gotten $5,000 for the car I bought a year earlier for $7,000, which means I could have had $8,000 to buy a one-year-old car for cash. Now let's compare that $9,000 car financed over four years at

$247 per month with the cash plan. That $9,000 car would have been worth $3,150 in four years after it was finally paid for. After four years on the finance plan, I would have had a $3,150 car, but on the cash plan I would have an $8,000 car fully paid. Which is the better plan?

While I do not recommend buying a car every year, we can see that the worst cash plan is better than the best financing plan. If I kept that eight-year-old $1,000 car for four years and saved $250 per month for four years, I would have had $12,000, not including interest.

Many people will ask if it is wise to buy older cars considering the cost of repairs. Let's analyze and see. If I buy a car on a finance plan, I am throwing interest money out the window. If I save on the cash plan, I have money coming in the window. When I add the finance interest I didn't have to pay to the savings interest, that total will go a long way toward paying for repairs on older cars. If I paid $3,840 in interest over four years and I earned 5 percent on my savings for four years (which would be $276), my total saved would be $4,116 available for repairs before it cost me anything.

Why don't more people use the cash plan? We

don't have money problems; we have ignorance problems and attitude problems about money and money matters. Ignorance—we have not been taught that the cash plan could be so much better. Attitude—we are too proud to drive the oldest car in the parking lot at work, and moreover, we lack discipline. We are not willing to discipline ourselves to save the $250 per month and not spend it for anything else. The cash plan works if we are willing to follow the plan.

Cost per Mile

The bottom line is this: How much does it cost you to drive from point A to point B? The cost per mile will tell you how much.

The way to determine the cost per mile is to add the sales price to the interest and divide that total by the projected number of years you plan to drive a particular car. Your answer will be the average cost per year. Then add the average projected cost per year for insurance, tags, gasoline, and repairs to the average cost per year to acquire the car and divide that total by the estimated miles per year you plan to drive. The answer will be the average cost per mile over the number of years you plan to drive it.

If you buy an expensive car and drive it few miles and trade often, the cost per mile could exceed $1 per mile, which exceeds the average person's budget guide for an auto. One dollar per mile times an average of 15,000 miles per year equals $15,000 per year, or $1,250 per month, to own and operate a car. If you drive only 10,000 miles per year at $1 per mile average, it would cost you $10,000 per year, or $833 per month, to own and operate a car. I strongly encourage you to compute how much it costs you per mile to drive each car you own. Do not take the estimated costs used by auto rental companies or the IRS, as each person's cost, interest, insurance, and repairs may differ.

9.

Sharing Your Resources: Strategies for Giving and Tithing on Any Budget

Our purpose as Christians is found in 1 Corinthians 10:31: "Whatsoever ye do, do all to the glory of God" (KJV). As Christians we should bring glory to God in every area of our lives, including the way we earn money, manage money, and give away money.

The way to honor God is to be obedient to God's Word and God's ways. What are God's ways of managing money? He first tells us to work hard and earn it honestly. Then He tells us to honor Him with the first part (10 percent). And finally, He tells us to save for the future, provide for our families, and give to the needy.

Our stewardship includes giving of our time, talent, and treasure. Most people find the easiest of these three to be our treasure. However, today, due to the economic problems we as a nation are experiencing, many people are not honoring God first in the giving of the tithe, and they are missing out on God's blessing that He promised us in

Malachi 3:10. God said we are robbing Him if we are not tithing—regularly giving God the first part of our income.

Proverbs 3:9 (TLB) instructs, "Honor the Lord by giving him the first part of all your income." The King James translation of this verse says, "Honour the LORD with thy substance, and with the firstfruits of all thine increase." God is telling us that we have two ways to honor Him. We can give to Him from what we already have, from our reserves, and we can give to Him from our increase. God also established the plan of regular systematic giving on the first day of the week. Now, God's Word does not say to honor the Lord by giving Him the first part of all your income *after taxes*. It does not say to honor the Lord by giving Him the first part of your income *unless you are in debt*, or *only if you are earning above poverty-level wages*, or *only as long as it is still tax deductible*. None of those conditions are part of God's plan. He says, "I want you to honor me regardless of the economic conditions of the land. And regardless of your personal situation, I want you to put Me first and honor Me." In Ephesians 6:2 (KJV), Paul tells us, "Honour thy father and mother." Children honor their parents by showing love to them through their obedience. Likewise, we honor God by showing our love for Him through our obedience.

We should give because we desire to honor the Lord. We have the freedom of choice to be obedient or to be disobedient. Proverbs 13:13 (TLB) says, "Despise God's Word and find yourself in trouble. Obey it and succeed." The consequences are that we will find ourselves in trouble if we continually choose to be disobedient to God, and we will have success if we choose to obey. God says that He wants us to bring the first part into the storehouse. He tells us in Malachi 3:10 (KJV), "Bring ye all the tithes into the storehouse [the tithe is a tenth; the storehouse is the church]. . .and prove me now." This is the only place in the Bible where God says, "Prove Me, try Me, test Me; see if I won't do what I tell you I will do." What does He say He will do? "[See] if I will not open you the windows of heaven, and pour you out a blessing, that there shall not be room enough to receive it." I believe God is saying, "I love you; you are My child; I want to bless you. The prerequisite is obedience, bringing that first part into the storehouse." He is saying that when we do that, He will know that we recognize that He is the owner and we are the managers, and that we choose to be obedient managers by returning the first part to Him. I believe God designed this plan to give us an opportunity for Him to bless the 90 percent or less that we keep.

God also tells us to give cheerfully: "Every man according as he purposeth in his heart, so let him give; not grudgingly, or of necessity: for God loveth a cheerful giver" (2 Corinthians 9:7 KJV). Moreover, we read that "it is more blessed to give than to receive" (Acts 20:35 KJV). To give any amount for any reason, we need to follow God's way to manage money; then we experience the greater blessing. But we are also told to give what we have, not what we don't have: "If you are really eager to give, then it isn't important how much you have to give. God wants you to give what you have, not what you haven't. Of course, I don't mean that those who receive your gifts should have an easy time of it at your expense" (2 Corinthians 8:12–13 TLB).

Give to the Needy

Paul exhorts us in Ephesians 4:28 (KJV), "Let him that stole steal no more: but rather let him labour, working with his hands the thing which is good, that he may have to give to him that needeth." We are to give not to the greedy but to the needy—those who can't help themselves.

If we are in a situation where we have a so-called financial problem, God is expecting us to do everything we can to manage well first. We are not needy until we have done everything we can do.

A lot of people are poor because they are lazy. Others are poor because they are poor managers. Still others are poor because they don't want to seek counsel. All they want is for somebody to give them a fish every day. They don't want someone to teach them to fish, because then they would have to go to work. We need to be sure in our budget planning that we do everything we can do God's way to help ourselves first. When we have done all we can, we need to trust God. God wants us to save so we can help each other.

Tips on Giving to Family and Friends

- Limit your gifts in number and amount per gift.
- Buy on a cash basis. Avoid using credit or credit cards.

- Make personal gifts (plaques, paintings, and poems, etc.).
- Make a written calendar list of known birthdays, anniversaries, and holidays; set a dollar amount for each based on your budget allocation for gifts; stick to your budget amount.
- Consider cards or letters in lieu of gifts.
- Consider baked goods as gifts when appropriate.
- In large families, draw names for exchanging gifts.
- Remember to honor the Lord at Christmas. It is His birthday. Find creative ways to honor the Lord.
- Have your children select a gift they would like, and then have them earn money to buy it and give it to a needy child their gender and age.
- Shop only by list for Christmas, predetermine the amount to spend on each gift, and stick to your list and amount.
- Mail packages early and use the least expensive carrier to deliver.

10.

The Decision to Borrow: Tips on Loans and Credit Cards

My counsel on the subject of borrowing is DO NOT BORROW! The overall purpose of this book is to encourage readers to get out of debt and to stay out of debt. It is possible! The process of becoming debt free always starts with a budget (a written plan) to increase income, reduce outgo, and control future spending so an abundance results that can be used to prepay debts and save for future purchases on a cash basis.

Realistically, however, we know that some people are not going to follow this process. So before doing any borrowing, the borrower must gather all the facts—the amount to borrow, the length of the loan, the interest rate, and the method of computing the interest. Also, one should know the amount of any late charges and penalties. If a borrower plans to prepay, they should know the method of computing the payoff or prepayment. Too many people enter into loan contracts without knowing and understanding the facts.

Credit Cards

Credit cards have been the means of overspending for many people, especially for persons with little discipline in controlling their spending. You can use credit cards two ways: as a convenience or as a necessity. If you pay your credit card bills in full every month, you are using them as a convenience. If you are unable to pay all credit cards in full every month, you are using them as a necessity. That is, you don't have the money at home or in the bank or in your pocket, and you can't make a purchase unless you use your credit card. We encourage every person who chooses to use credit cards to pay them in full every month and to use them only as a convenience.

When you pay your credit cards in full every month you avoid the interest, which is usually very high in comparison to other types of loans. Using credit cards is convenient, but no one needs to use them. One can cash checks, buy merchandise, and even rent cars without credit cards. (Yes, I've done it several times in the past.)

A credit card is an easy way to buy now and pay later, but it is a form of borrowing money, and often, a finance charge will be added to your bill each month on the balance you still owe. How much you pay for the use of credit cards depends on three terms of the credit card contract. Creditors must tell you (1) the annual percentage rate (APR), (2) the method of calculating the finance charge, and (3) when the finance charge begins.

On any loan, the interest or finance charge depends on the amount you owe, the interest rate, the length of the loan, and the method of calculating the interest or finance charge.

Many creditors in the past did not start a finance charge until the first day of the next billing period, which gave you an "interest free float." You need to read your renewal contracts carefully, as many creditors are now starting to compute interest as of the date of purchase and may back out the interest only if the bill is paid in full by the due date, usually ten to fifteen days. Another caution is to avoid those credit cards that offer lower interest rates but tie their variable rate to the prime rate. If the prime rate goes up, so does your credit card rate. Also, read the fine print on credit card offers of a low or no rate for a period of time to get your business, as most of them will jump your interest rate if you are late or pay less than the minimum amount. Some of the higher rates may be as high as 29 percent.

Auto Loans

Our first encouragement is to buy only cars that you can pay for in cash without financing. If you decide to finance a car, get all the facts about the contract before buying. Pay as much down as possible, and borrow for the shortest period of time that your budget will permit. Obtain both the interest rate and the method of computing it. Simple interest on the unpaid balance is the best method for the borrower. You pay interest only on the amount of money you owe each month. This is the same method used for most home mortgages. Another method is the "add-on" method, where interest is computed on the full amount of the loan for the full period of the loan, and the total of the principle and interest is divided by the number of payments scheduled to repay the debt. In this method, you are paying interest on money that has already been repaid.

Another fact you need to obtain before borrowing for an auto loan is the method used to determine the payoff, should you decide to prepay the loan from your surplus or from the sale of the car. On "simple interest" loans, the balance and the payoff figures would be the same, with only the daily interest to the exact date of payoff

111

being added. This should be less than thirty days' interest. With "add-on" interest loans, various methods may be used, with one of the more popular methods being the "rule of 78s." This is a short-rate rebate method that gives you back only a portion of your prefigured and precharged interest. With the add-on interest type loan and the rule of 78s pay-off method, even if you pay off the loan in half the time, you do not get half the interest back. Remember, every dollar you pay in interest is money thrown away.

Housing Debt

In 1928, 98 percent of the people who bought a home paid cash; only 2 percent financed their homes. In only forty years, by 1968, only 2 percent of the people who bought a home paid cash, and 98 percent financed their homes. Only a few families today would be able to pay cash for a home. We encourage you to pay all cash if you can. If you can't, put down the most you can and finance the balance over the shortest period of time your budget permits. Then try to prepay your mortgage to get out of debt faster. Your ultimate goal should be to be debt free as soon as possible.

When you shop for a mortgage on your home, get all the facts: the amount you will need as a down payment, the amount you will need to borrow, the total amount of closing costs and fees, the interest rate, the method of computing the interest, the length of the loan, and the amount of monthly payments. Also, does the lender have a prepayment penalty or prepayment privilege? Get the estimated closing date and the amount you need to take to closing, also the type of payment required at closing (usually a cashier's check).

There are a variety of mortgage loans to choose from: conventional, FHA, VA, reverse, and negative amortization. Avoid a negative amortized loan. FHA (Federal Housing Administration) and VA (Veterans Affairs) loans are usually designed for sales with low down payments, and we encourage large down payments when you buy a home.

With FHA loans and other high-percentage loans to value, an extra insurance fee is usually charged to help cover the lender's higher risk. You can avoid this additional cost by making a larger down payment. We encourage you to avoid "interest only" loans, because you will be unable to get out of debt or ever have your house paid off. God told us two thousand years ago to "owe no man any thing."

A reverse mortgage is designed for those over age sixty-two who have equity in their home, who want to stay in their home but need greater income. If their home has a small mortgage or no mortgage, the reverse mortgage pays off any existing mortgage and starts making a monthly payment to them. That eliminates them making a mortgage payment, and the monthly payments they receive are not taxable income by the IRS.

Time = Interest

Acknowledge the importance of the length of time over which you repay the loan. The longer the time, the more the cost. When you prepay any amount at any time on your existing mortgage, it will shorten the time it takes to pay off the loan, and it will save you an amazing amount of interest. You don't have to take thirty years to pay off a thirty-year loan. By prepaying, you could shorten a thirty-year loan to eight, ten, twelve, or fifteen years, depending on the amount and the frequency of prepayments. We suggest that you discuss your prepayment plans with your lender to be sure that the prepayment amounts will be applied directly to the principle and thereby reduce the next month's interest. Prepayments can be made monthly, quarterly, yearly, or any way you desire. The larger the amount and the more frequently they are made, the more you save in interest.

Personal Loans

Personal loans can be obtained from a variety of sources with differing terms. Most personal loans fall into the unsecured type—that is, without any collateral pledged. Some secured loans are also in the personal-loan category. The same caution is given as with all other loans. Get the facts, evaluate the options, and do not rush into borrowing until you have time to pray about it and receive peace about it from God.

Personal loans from small loan companies usually carry a higher interest rate than most credit cards. Bank interest rates on personal loans can be slightly lower than most credit cards. Credit unions usually charge less than banks. Personal loans on your whole-life insurance policy will often have the lowest interest rate. Interest rates change from time to time and from location to location, so the best way to know which is best for you is to get the facts from all sources before making any decisions.

Nowhere in the Bible does it say to go to the bank or to the government when you need help. Instead, we read in 1 Timothy 5:8 (TLB), "Anyone who won't care for his own relatives when they need help, especially those living in his own family, has no right to say he is a Christian." God is telling us that family should help family. Thus, we should help our own relatives when they need help. We need to manage well so that we have an abundance and can help our family from our abundance. Do you have a relative in need?

Let us assume you have a relative paying 18 percent average interest on credit cards, and you are receiving 4 percent interest on your savings. If their debts total $10,000 at 18 percent, and you have a surplus of $10,000 and you agree to lend them $10,000 at 6 percent interest, guess what just happened? You helped them save 12 percent, and they helped you earn 2 percent more. In this type of personal loan, both gain and no one loses (except for the credit card company). When both needs are met, God receives glory. The terms for every loan to a relative should be made in writing and repaid as agreed.

When making a loan to a relative, you need to use the same wisdom and judgment as if you were lending someone else's money, because you are—you are lending what belongs to God, because He owns it all. If you lend to those who mismanage money, they will continue to mismanage money unless they receive wisdom from God and change their attitudes about spending, borrowing, and living within their income.

We encourage you to look for evidence of responsibility before you lend to a relative. A Chinese proverb says, "You can give a boy a fish and tomorrow he is hungry, but if you teach him how to fish, he can have food for life." What is more valuable to the boy? Obviously, it is more valuable to know how to fish. The same is true with money. It is more valuable to know how to manage money than to receive money every day. Be sure you offer the wisdom to know how to manage money before you lend to a relative. This book given as a gift is a great place to start in helping them.

If you are the one in need, follow all the steps in this book and do everything you can to increase your income, lower outgo, and control future spending. This may mean selling assets and

making sacrifices. When you have done everything you can, pray for God to give you peace
about sharing your need with a family member
or relative. When you have that peace, don't ask
them for money. Simply ask for their permission
to share your circumstances with them, as you
would like their advice. What would they do if
they were in your position? They may give you
several options; they may even offer to help you.

If they don't help you with a loan, thank them
and love them just the same. Then continue to
pray for God's direction for your next step.

If God does not supply your need through a
loan consolidation, He may want you to learn by
working it out the hard way—month by month
with each creditor. God knows that some people
need to learn the hard way. According to a survey,
75 percent of those who obtained a loan consolidation ended up right back where they were in
twelve months' time because they did not overcome ignorance with wisdom and did not change
their attitude about spending, borrowing, and
living within their income.

11.

Cutting Costs: Some Simple Money-Saving Hints

Housing
Mortgage

- Consider renting part of your home to someone else.
- Consider possible refinancing to lower your interest rate and lower your payment.

Rent

- Shop for lower rental payments.
- Consider renting part of your home to someone else.

Home Insurance

- Shop and compare for the best possible terms and rates.
- Do not overpay to your mortgage escrow account for home insurance.

- Consider increasing the deductible amount.

Real Estate Taxes

- Compare the real estate tax assessor's appraisal of your home with other comparable home values. If you are overassessed, ask for a reconsideration.
- Do not overpay to your mortgage escrow account for real estate taxes.

Electric/Gas/Oil

- Check attic for insulation, doors and windows for air leaks, and change filters regularly.
- Keep thermostat set at moderate comfort levels.
- Delay using heat or cool air until necessary. Use sweaters, blankets, or fans.
- Close off any part of the home not used frequently.
- Turn off unused lights; reduce bulb wattage in nonwork or nonreading areas.
- Group bath times to conserve hot water.

- Insulate all exposed hot water lines and your hot water heater.
- Reduce your hot water heater thermostat(s) from 140 to 120 degrees.
- Reduce the number of hours you heat hot water (manually or with a timer).
- Avoid partial-load use of dishwasher, washer, and dryer—use a full load.
- Stop dishwasher before drying cycle—allow dishes to dry by themselves.
- Group your cooking and baking while stove and oven are hot.
- Consider solar energy to heat water.

Telephone

- Evaluate need for more than one home phone and for cell phones.
- Use plain standard phone, no frills, no extra features.
- Limit the number and length of all long-distance calls.
- Make long-distance calls during reduced rate times.
- Write more letters and make fewer long-distance calls.

Water and Sewage

- Conserve use of water when washing dishes and hands and brushing teeth.
- Conserve use of water when bathing (shorter showers).
- Use well water when and where applicable.
- Turn off hose when not needed to wash cars, boat, and house.
- Repair all leaks promptly.

Maintenance

- Do your own house and lawn pest control.
- Reduce use of fertilizer—use natural organic materials.
- Do your own plumbing, electric, carpentry, and other repairs.
- Mow, edge, trim, and maintain your own lawn.
- Rent the equipment and clean your own carpets and furniture.
- Do your own painting and wallpapering.

Cable TV

- Consider using standard local stations only.
- Next consider using the basic cable only.
- Avoid "Pay for View" and unnecessary extra-tier channels.

Furniture

- Shop for best buys—sales, discontinued items.
- Consider repairing, refinishing, and recovering used good-quality furniture.
- Shop the local shopper's guide, garage sales, and thrift stores.
- Consider making your own furniture.

Appliances

- Maintain what you have—consult service manuals.
- Keep written maintenance charts.
- Do not overload or abuse appliances. Follow instructions.
- Learn to be a do-it-yourselfer. Seek counsel when available.

- Before replacing, consider a repair or over-haul. Many older units are better quality and cost less to repair.
- If replacing, use a buyer's guide to determine the best manufacturer.
- Stick to standard models. More dials and gadgets usually cost more and require more maintenance.
- Shop and compare price, quality, and service. Keep a written record.
- Look for high-volume dealers who carry name-brand products under their own label at lower prices.
- Buy on a cash basis. Avoid trade-ins. Seek discounts for cash.
- Avoid dealer service contracts—usually expensive and no guarantee that they will be in business when you are in need.
- Seek free delivery and installation.
- Look for similar used units in the newspaper or shopper's guide.

Food

- Shop by a written list only—prepared at home.

- Buy larger quantities, which usually cost less per ounce.
- Shop less frequently—every week or every two weeks.
- Avoid buying when hungry.
- Leave children and spouse at home.
- Only use coupons for items on your need list.
- Only use coupons after shopping for price—not label.
- Shop for price per serving. Compare canned, frozen, and fresh.
- Reduce or eliminate paper products.
- Compare the price of drugstore-type items at food stores with discount chain stores. Usually, but not always, they are cheaper at discount stores.
- Avoid sugar-coated higher priced cereals. They are usually more expensive but not more nutritious.
- Avoid prepared foods, TV dinners, pot-pies, cakes. You are paying more for expensive labor that you can supply.
- Avoid food plans that package and deliver large quantities of meats. You will end up eating more meat, which in the long run

will cost you more, especially if you buy their overpriced freezer to go with it.

- Compare store-brand prices with the more popular brands.
- Buy items when in season to get the lowest prices.
- Shop for advertised specials but be sure products really are "on sale," not just "as advertised" but the same old price.
- Consider making your own baby food.
- Consider canning your own fresh vegetables.
- Consider buying in bulk with other families.
- Consider serving your family "restaurant style" not family style—only one plate per meal filled in the kitchen—no extra food on the table.
- Consider buying items advertised as buy one, get one free—if it is on your list or an item you frequently use that has a long shelf life.

Auto

- Learn to perform your own routine maintenance—oil change, lubrication, etc.

126

- Perform preventative maintenance over the more costly corrective maintenance.
- Purchase your parts and supplies from wholesale distributors for the best grades and prices.
- Maintain a written regular maintenance chart or list for every car to extend the life of your cars (up to 40 percent).
- Consider buying "take-off" tires from dealers who frequently change tires on new cars or on fleets of cars.
- Use the cheapest fuel rated for your car.
- Buy only what you can pay for in cash—avoid financing.
- Consider repairing your old car, as the cost of repairs is almost always cheaper than buying and financing a new car.
- If it is really time to buy another car, consider a newer but less expensive car. Many cars can be bought for half the price when three to four years old.
- Before buying any car, new or newer than your present car, check your budget to see how much cash you have and how much you can afford to pay monthly.
- Avoid buying another car if your present

car is not paid in full. That leads to upside-down financing and additional costs of refinancing, especially if the payoff is computed on the rule of 78s.

- Realize that it is usually better to bargain for a discount on the purchase of your new car and pay cash for it than to buy on the "trade-in" plan.

- If you do finance your new car purchase, shop for the best financing available, not just the quickest and easiest offered by the dealer.

- If you buy a used car, talk to the previous owner before you buy. Also have it checked by your mechanic before you buy.

- Bargain for a short-term 100 percent guarantee if you buy a used car.

- Avoid being pressured by sales tactics. Set your own price and car type desired and stick to your plan, even if it means walking away from a so-called good deal that requires a quick decision.

- Be willing to accept minor problems or repairs on older cars.

- Avoid buying a new model when they first come out. It is better to wait for a demonstrator or year-end closeout sale.

- Note that the standard model usually provides the same transportation as the luxury model and at a substantial savings.
- Avoid the use of credit life insurance. It is expensive and unnecessary if you have an adequate overall insurance program.
- Note that extended warranties are also expensive and should not be necessary if you are buying a quality car.
- The average family should avoid new car leasing, as it is always more expensive in the long run. If you can't afford a down payment, you most likely can't afford the car.

Insurance
Life

- Seek godly counsel to establish an overall insurance plan for your present income and your specific needs and goals. GET THE FACTS!
- Establish a budget to determine how much insurance you need. GET THE FACTS!

- Select a plan that meets your needs and fits your budget. GET THE FACTS!
- Get godly counsel from several qualified people, but recognize that you are responsible for your decision. Decide after getting the facts and praying for God's direction, which usually comes in the form of a lasting peace about your decision.
- Buy insurance to provide for your family if you are unable to provide from your estate, which is your abundance.

Health

- Again, seek godly counsel.
- Determine your need.
- Get the facts!
- Select a plan that fits your income and need.
- Buy what you can afford and need.
- Consider a major medical plan that insures the big-ticket liability, not every pill and every doctor visit, unless you can afford the low-deductible all-expenses-paid policy offered by your insurance company.

Debts

- Establish a plan to get out and stay out of debt.
- Stop using credit cards, except for convenience, and pay the balance IN FULL every month.
- Decide to pay cash from this day on.
- Save for the future at the same time you are paying off your debts.
- Be fair to every creditor. Pay each one every dollar.
- Do not leave any creditor out of your current plan.
- If you are past due with any creditor, contact them, apologize for breaking your promise to pay the minimum required amount, and advise them of your plan to repay all past-due payments—and make all future required payments on time as agreed. Then keep your promise and follow your plan.
- Make as many sacrifices as necessary to follow your plan until you are current with all creditors.
- Seek options to increase your income,

lower your outgo, and control your future spending until you reach your goals.

Entertainment and Recreation

Dining Out

- Dine out less frequently and at less expensive places.
- Order only water to drink and avoid the expensive beverages when eating out.
- Use discount, early-bird, or two-for-one specials when they fit your time and budget plan.
- Establish your budget and the specific amount you have allocated for dining out. Then select a plan of places to go and limits to pay.

Trips/Vacation

- Plan vacations during off-season, if possible, when rates are lower.
- Consider camping to avoid higher motel and restaurant costs.

- Select vacations close to home; they give you more time to recreate and cost less for travel.
- Consider swapping your house with a relative or a Christian family in another town for your vacation.
- Stay at home and change the daily routine and activities for the entire family.
- If flying, plan in advance and buy super-saver tickets or special fare plans.
- Consider a working vacation where the whole family spends part of every day painting the house or doing some other project together.

Babysitting

- Find one or more couples with children and trade off babysitting for each other at no cost.
- Barter for sitters. You fix their hair or mow their lawn; they sit for your children.

Activities

- Plan activities like hiking, camping,

swimming at the lake or beach, etc. that have minimum expense.

- Attend movies, bowling, or other activities during hours of lower admission fees.
- Get two or more families together to share video rentals.
- Carpool to nearby towns for special sporting events.
- Volunteer to help serve food at children's school sports events and get free admission.
- Swap your boat for your friend's camper for a week.

Clothing

- Make some clothing for you and the children as time and talent permit.
- Buy from a need list only, prepared at home after looking in the closets.
- Buy during the "off" season when prices are their lowest.
- Buy basic outfits that you can mix and match, dress up or dress down.
- Shop at discount outlets and for special sales.

- Buy hand- and machine-washable fabrics to avoid dry cleaning costs.
- Repair any damaged clothing early.
- Take good care of your existing clothing.
- Pass hand-me-downs among friends and family.
- Shop garage sales and thrift stores for real bargains.

Savings

- Use an automatic withdrawal (payroll deduction) when possible.
- Pay your savings account just as you would a creditor.
- Save for a purpose. Set your goals. Start saving NOW.
- Set a fixed amount to be saved regularly, based on your budget.
- Possible savings goals: to build an estate; to buy a home, car, furniture, appliance; to take a vacation; to make a home or auto repair; to be able to help others with a gift or loan.
- Save one specific amount for the future— not to be spent.

- Save another specific amount as a reserve to be spent for the variety of other purposes you are saving.

Investments

- The purpose of every investment should be to bring glory to God.
- Investments are longer-term savings usually for a specific purpose, such as pensions, college education, etc.
- Use automatic withdrawal (payroll deduction) when possible.
- Set a fixed amount to be invested based on your budget.
- One type of investment provides you with an income now.
- Another type of investment simply grows and only provides you with the increase when sold.
- Some investment earnings are taxable now.
- Other investment earnings are tax deferred.
- Some investments are made through financial institutions. Other investments are made direct to individuals.

- Where applicable, both husband and wife should agree on the investments before they are made.
- Every investment has a degree of risk.
- Every investor should seek a balance between convenience, availability, rate of return, and safety.
- Do not invest in anything you don't understand.
- Consider investing in your own family.
- One of your best investments is to get out of debt.

Medical Expenses

- Take good care of yourself and your family. Preventative action is less expensive than corrective action.
- Select physicians and dentists who practice preventative care.
- Get estimates of costs in advance. When practical, get second opinions.
- Shop for price on prescriptions, glasses, etc.
- Read books and articles on proper health care and nutrition.

Miscellaneous

Drugstore Items

- Shop for price on each item and from various type sources; compare grocery stores, drugstores, discount stores, direct sales, etc.
- Always shop from a needs list prepared at home after looking in all your closets.
- Compare price per ounce or per unit and buy the larger quantity or size when it proves to be the best buy.

Beauty Parlor/Barber Shop

- Do your hair care at home when possible; trim your spouse's hair in between haircuts, and learn to cut your children's hair.
- Stretch the time between hair appointments.

Laundry/Dry Cleaners

- Buy clothing that doesn't need to be dry cleaned.
- Use coin-operated dry clean machines when available.

- Use full loads, not partial and not overloaded, in coin-operated laundry machines.
- Buy your own washer and dryer as soon as possible, even used, as it is cheaper to do laundry yourself at home.
- Dry your own clothes on a line in lieu of a dryer.

Lunch

- Pack lunch for your children and yourself.
- Drink only water for lunch.
- Avoid buying special lunch-size pack-aged foods that are usually very expensive. Make and package your own.
- Use reusable containers for packing lunches. Avoid more expensive throwaways.

Allowances

- Avoid allowances. Only reward children for extra work performed, not the usual expected chores, such as picking up their clothes, cleaning their rooms, helping with dishes, etc., which is part of their responsibility as a member of the family.

- Give your children an opportunity to work and earn money. Select special projects, such as washing windows, washing and waxing the car, mowing the lawn, and babysitting, etc. to earn money in lieu of a set allowance for doing nothing.

Subscriptions

- Reduce or eliminate periodical subscriptions (paper, magazines, books, records, etc.).
- If a subscription is continued, use longer-term contracts (two to three years), which are usually less expensive.
- Swap subscriptions with neighbors, friends, or family.

Education

- Determine the amount available based on your budget.
- Gather the facts about all the options.

- Decide on the school based on the best academically that your budget can afford.
- Save in advance. Avoid borrowing for education.
- Have your student participate in the expense by working part-time job(s), especially for college education.
- Evaluate need for, value of, and interest in special lessons—music, dance, etc.
- Seek scholarships and grants that may be available.
- Carpool to reduce transportation costs when applicable.
- Buy used books in lieu of new books when available.
- Have your student avoid owning a car while in college, if possible.
- Teach your college student to establish and live on a budget.
- Do not allow your student to use credit cards.

Pocket Money

- Set a regular specific amount, weekly, based on the budget.

- Stick to that amount.
- Avoid impulse spending for drinks, snacks, gum, etc.
- Decide in advance what to buy with your pocket money.
- Avoid being wasteful or buying unnecessary items.
- Milk, bread, gas, etc. are not considered miscellaneous pocket money items. These already have specific budget categories.

Pet Store/Veterinarian

- Consider the cost of keeping a pet before buying.
- Limit your purchases to the pet's needs and your budget.
- Shop for best veterinarian fees.
- Have children participate in providing for their pet care.

Other

- Shop for the best bank services. Avoid service charges.
- Learn to prepare your own income taxes.

- Shop for fees if you need to use an attorney.
- Shop for child-care rates. Consider bartering.
- Keep the required minimum balance in your checking account to avoid service charges and returned check fees.
- Carry no credit cards, checks, or extra cash unless you have a planned purchase that day.

Learning by Example: How a Real-Life Couple Balanced Their Budget

Before counseling, Bob and Sue's outgo exceeded their income by $610 per month. Plus they took an average of $74 per month from their savings and borrowed $1,200 just to make ends meet. In addition, they were increasing their debt by using credit cards. While they wanted to give 10 percent to God, they were only giving 3 percent. They wanted to increase their savings, but they were spending part of their existing savings.

Obviously many changes needed to take place in the next year if they were going to accomplish their goals, which were to honor the Lord with 10 percent, get out of debt, stay out of debt, provide for the family, and save for the future. After counseling they overcame their ignorance by learning God's wisdom on managing money. Next came a major decision on their part: "Are we going to apply God's direction in our daily financial plan? If so, we need to change our attitude about money and money matters."

They learned God's way to manage money

and made the decision to change their attitude and obey God's way. The following paragraphs indicate the step-by-step decisions they made that resulted in a balanced budget that enhanced their love, joy, peace, and contentment as they worked toward their goals.

Income

After Bob and Sue's decision to change their attitude about borrowing, spending, and living within their income, God began to bless them. Bob received a 10 percent increase in his salary. Sue received an increase of $2,076 per year. They also decided not to borrow any more money and not to plan on any more gifts to meet their budget needs. After reviewing their tax withholding, they lowered the amount withheld on their W-4 forms so they would eliminate their usual tax refund. They realized that the refund could be better used payday by payday to balance their budget. Because they were going to increase their savings on a regular basis with their new plan, the interest they would earn would increase from $5 per month to $10 per month. The net income from all sources would increase from $3,000 to $3,130 per month.

Outgo

1. Bob and Sue immediately started to give 10 percent of their gross income to God—from $90 per month to $313 per month, an increase of $2,676 per year.

2. They did a projected tax return at the beginning of the year and lowered their withholding to plan for an estimated break-even point so there would be no refund and no amount owed for the next filing period. Even with an increase in taxable income of $4,224, they could reduce their withholding from $444 to $437 per month.

3. They refinanced their home at a lower interest rate and lowered the payment from $621 to $421 per month. They also paid all past-due payments and paid off the auto loan in full from the refinance proceeds. They also shopped for a better rate on their homeowner's insurance policy and reduced the premium from $384 to $336 per year. They projected an increase of $24 in their real estate tax. They estimated that they could reduce their electric bill from $107 to $97 per month by lowering their hot water thermostat and installing a timer to heat it only when they needed it hot. They decided to reduce the number and length of long-distance calls to cut the phone bill in half,

from $62 to $36 per month. The water bill and the trash removal rates were set rates, so no change could be made in those two items. They decided to do more of the house maintenance themselves and reduce the expense from $41 to $36 per month. It was a hard decision, but they canceled cable TV and eliminated the $23 per month expense. They also decided to get by with their present furniture and not spend any money next year on furniture, which eliminated $32 per month. The net result of all their changes in the housing category resulted in a reduction from $1,068 to $770 per month, or a savings of $3,576 per year.

4. Bob and Sue started shopping for food by a list prepared at home and then stuck to their list. They also used coupons, but only for the items already on the list. Before using any coupons, they shopped for the best price of other brands, including the store-brand products. They also changed their diets by reducing the purchase of snacks and drinks, and they decided washing dishes was cheaper than buying paper cups and plates. The end result was a reduction of $31 per month, or $372 per year, at the grocery store.

5. One of their tougher decisions was whether to sell an auto and eliminate the auto

payment of $288 per month or to borrow $6,912 more on their home refinance to pay off the auto loan. They decided to borrow $6,912 more on the home to eliminate the auto payment. This allowed them to take a greater interest deduction on their tax return. They also decided to reduce their unnecessary driving and combine all their shopping to one time per week or on their way to or from work to lower the cost for gasoline from $96 to $84 per month. They also shopped for a better rate on auto insurance and lowered their premium from $288 to $222 for a six-month premium. Bob also decided to do some of the minor auto repairs himself to lower their auto maintenance expense by an estimated $192 per year. The net result of their changes in the auto category reduced their expenses by $327 per month, or $3,924 per year.

6. They made no change on their life or health insurance but decided to trust the Lord and canceled their disability insurance, which saved them $132 per year.

7. They decided to take $2,229 from the home refinance and pay all past-due payments in the All Other Debt category. This paid in full a credit card balance and a debt to a doctor, which

were both due in full. In an effort to get out of debt as soon as possible, they decided to prepay by $144 per month on the remaining debts in the All Other Debt category. Their plan was to pay $427 per month instead of the contracted amount of $283 per month.

8. As they analyzed their entertainment and recreation activities, they agreed to dine out less often and cut back slightly on their vacation. When they cut back on their evening out activities, doing so also cut back on the babysitter expense. They also decided to reduce their video rentals by 50 percent. The hard decision was to sell the boat to eliminate all boat expenses. Their net reduction in the entertainment and recreation category was $876 per year.

9. To cut back on their clothing expense, they decided to buy only what they absolutely needed and to shop for bargain sales and shop at discount shops. They were amazed at how little they really "needed" when they took inventory of their closet and dresser drawers. They decided to stop any impulse buying and browsing for clothes. Their projected savings in this category was $120 per year.

10. Bob and Sue knew the trend had to be

reversed in the savings category. Last year they took out $888, which averaged $74 per month. The guideline amount to save for their level of income was $116 per month, but they put a higher priority on getting out of debt, so they prepaid their All Other Debt category by $144 per month and cut back their monthly savings from $116 to $54 per month. Another reason was that they already had an existing savings balance of $1,200. Their net change in savings was from taking out $74 per month to adding $54 per month, which was an effective increase of $128 per month, or $1,536 per year.

11. While the guideline amount to invest was $185 per month for their level of income, they decided to defer any investments until they paid off all debts in the All Other Debt category of $8,378 and had an amount in their savings equal to three months' gross income ($3,130 x 3 = $9,390). They estimated two years to pay off the $8,378 and another year to achieve their savings goal.

12. While Bob and Sue's medical expenses were normally low due to their good health, the past year was higher than usual, primarily due to the stress brought on by their financial pressures.

Now that the financial pressures were removed with their new budget, they reduced their projected expense for medical from $87 to $35 per month, or a reduction of $624 per year.

13. In the Miscellaneous category, they made changes where they could. They cut back on their drugstore item spending and decided to trim hair at home between haircuts at the shop. They decided to carry their lunch more often to reduce their lunch-money spending. They discontinued magazine subscriptions and cut gift buying to nearly one-half of their previous spending. They also cut their pocket money spending by one-half. Their final cutback was to find another home for their pet. The net reduction of Miscellaneous spending was $116 per month, or $1,392 per year.

As you can see, it took the knowledge of a guide, the wisdom of godly counsel, the changed attitudes of Bob and Sue, and finally their commitment to establish a plan (the budget) and to follow the plan before the problem was solved. It didn't happen overnight! It took one day at a time, one decision after another, and one item at a time to balance the budget.

Bob and Sue found out that biblical principles applied to everyday finances really work!

They were banking on the Bible for a balanced budget, and it happened. It was all here, in *Your Money in Tough Times*, and it is here for you. May God bless you richly for your obedience to His Word and His ways to manage money.

AVERAGE MONTHLY INCOME AND OUTGO FOR THE PAST CALENDAR YEAR

PAST   PROJECTED   FROM _____ TO _____

GROSS INCOME PER MONTH _____ [ ]   **7. Debts** _____ [ ] ●
  Salary, Pension, Soc Sec (His) ____ [ ]   Credit Cards _____ [ ]
  Salary, Pension, Soc Sec (Hers) ____ [ ]   Installment Loans _____ [ ]
  Interest and dividends ____ [ ]   Other _____ _____ [ ]
  Net from Investments/Rents ____ [ ]   **8. Enter/Recreation** _____ [ ]
  Gifts and Inheritance ____ [ ]   Dining Out _____ [ ]
  Tax Refunds ____ [ ]   Trips / Vacation _____ [ ]
  Other _____ ____ [ ]   Babysitters _____ [ ]

OUTGO PER MONTH   Activities _____ [ ]
1. Tithe and Offering _____ [ ]   Video Rentals _____ [ ]
2. Taxes (IRS - Soc. Sec.-Med.) _____ [ ]   Other _____ _____ [ ]
NET SPENDABLE INCOME _____ [ ]   **9. Clothing (Cash)** _____ [ ]
(GROSS INCOME MINUS LINES 1 & 2)
ALSO LIST ON LINE A BELOW)   **10. Savings (+or-)** _____ [ ] ●
                                                 11. Investments (+or-) _____ [ ] ●
3. Housing _____ [ ]   **12. Medical Expenses**
  Mortgage (Rent) ____ [ ]   Doctor _____ [ ]
  House Insurance ____ [ ]   Dentist _____ [ ]
  Real Estate Taxes ____ [ ]   Prescriptions _____ [ ]
  Electricity / Gas / Oil ____ [ ]   Other _____ _____ [ ]
  Telephone ____ [ ]   **13. Miscellaneous**
  Water & Sewage ____ [ ]   Drugstore Items _____ [ ]
  Trash Removal ____ [ ]   Beauty / Barber _____ [ ]
  Maintenance ____ [ ]   Laundry / Dry Cleaning _____ [ ]
  Cable TV ____ [ ]   Lunch (Work / School) _____ [ ]
  Other _____ ____ [ ]   Subscriptions _____ [ ]
4. Food (Grocery Store) _____ [ ]   Gifts (incl Christmas) _____ [ ]
5. Auto (Transportation)   Special Education _____ [ ]
  Payments ____ [ ]   Pocket Money _____ [ ]
  Gas ____ [ ]   Pet Store / Veterinarian _____ [ ]
  Auto Insurance ____ [ ]   Other _____ _____ [ ]
  License Tag ____ [ ]
  Repairs / Maintenance ____ [ ]   **TOTAL EXPENSES (3-13)** _____ [ ]
  Vehicle Replacement ____ [ ]   (ALSO LIST ON LINE B BELOW)
6. Insurance _____ [ ]   **A. NET SPENDABLE INCOME** _____ [ ]
  Life ____ [ ]   **B. LESS EXPENSES (3-13)** _____ [ ]
  Health ____ [ ]   **C. DIFFERENCE/MONTH (+OR-)** _____ [ ]
  Other _____ ____ [ ]   (LINE A MINUS LINE B)
                                               D. DIFFERENCE/YEAR (+OR-) _____ [ ]
                                               (MULTIPLY LINE C X 12)

INSTRUCTIONS:
Insert only "Past" income and outgo on the lines – After Chapter 7 insert only "Projected" income and outgo in the boxes.
Use Pencil --- Use the most accurate figures possible—Fill every blank, if no amount insert a dash (—).
Round all figures off to the nearest dollar (941.36 should be 941) (941.82 should be 942).
Convert all weekly figures to monthly ($100/wk x 52 wks = $5,200/yr ÷ 12 mo = $433/mo.
If self-employed do NOT include business and use only your net profit from the business that was brought
home for the family use.
● Do these 3 projections last and divide your abundance among them.

FORM #1

153

LIST OF DEBTS

as of _____

date prepared

	1 TO WHOM OWED	2 USED FOR WHAT	3 CURRENT UNPAID BALANCE	4 DOLLAR AMOUNT PAST DUE	5 CONTRACT MONTHLY PAYMENT	6 INTEREST RATE (APR)
HOUSING (Primary home only)						
1						
2						
3						

HOUSING TOTAL ⟶

AUTO (Do Not Include Business Vehicles)						
1						
2						
3						

AUTO TOTAL ⟶

ALL OTHER DEBTS (List from the largest balance down to the smallest balance)

1						
2						
3						
4						
5						
6						
7						
8						
9						
10						
11						
12						
13						
14						
15						
16						
17						
18						
19						
20						
21						
22						
23						
24						

ALL OTHER DEBTS TOTAL ⟶
(Do **NOT** include housing and auto total in this total)

INSTRUCTIONS: Use pencil—Round all figures to the nearest dollar.
If self-employed do NOT include business debts.
You should have 3 separate totals for the 3 different categories of debt.

FORM #2

MONTHLY BUDGET GUIDE

Date Completed _____

A. **PROJECTED** GROSS AVERAGE **MONTHLY** INCOME (from form #1) $ [   ]

B. **PROJECTED** GROSS **ANNUAL** INCOME (Line A x 12) $ [   ]

BUDGET CATEGORIES	1.	FROM PERCENTAGE GUIDE	2.	from Line A GROSS MONTHLY INCOME	3.	YOUR GUIDE (nearest dollar)	4.
1. Tithe (God)		_____ % X		$_____ =		$_____	
2. Taxes (Gov't)		_____ % X		$_____ =		$_____	

C.   TOTAL OF CATEGORIES 1. & 2. = $ _____

D. NET SPENDABLE INCOME (Line A minus Line C) $ [   ]

BUDGET CATEGORIES	FROM PERCENTAGE GUIDE	from Line D NET MONTHLY INCOME	YOUR GUIDE (nearest dollar)
3. Housing	_____ % X	$_____ =	$_____
4. Food	_____ % X	$_____ =	$_____
5. Auto	_____ % X	$_____ =	$_____
6. Insurance	_____ % X	$_____ =	$_____
7. Debts	_____ % X	$_____ =	$_____
8. Enter/Recreation	_____ % X	$_____ =	$_____
9. Clothing	_____ % X	$_____ =	$_____
10. Savings	_____ % X	$_____ =	$_____
11. Investment	_____ % X	$_____ =	$_____
12. Medical	_____ % X	$_____ =	$_____
13. Miscellaneous	_____ % X	$_____ =	$_____

E. NET SPENDABLE TOTAL (Total of Categories 3-13, should equal line D.) $ [   ]

INSTRUCTIONS:
Use pencil. Use nearest dollar amount. Use **gross monthly income** in column 3 for categories 1 & 2. Use **net spendable income** in column 3 for categories 3-13. Gross incomes below $30,000 do **NOT** have a percentage in the investment category. Use the best estimate for your projected gross average monthly income on Line A. This is NOT YOUR budget, or your limit, only a guide for your income level. DO NOT change any percent from the guide.

FORM #3

BUDGET ANALYSIS

Date Completed _____

COLUMN	1	2	3	4	5
	PAST MONTHLY BUDGET (FROM FORM #1)	MONTHLY BUDGET GUIDE (FROM FORM #4)	DIFFERENCE (SUBTRACT COLUMN 2 FROM COLUMN 1) + IF OVER GUIDE - IF UNDER GUIDE	order of difference	PROJECTED MONTHLY BUDGET
A. GROSS MONTHLY INCOME	$	$			$
1. TITHE (God) (OFFERINGS)					
2. TAXES (Gov't) (IRS - SS - MED)					
B. NET SPENDABLE INCOME (GROSS MINUS CATEGORIES 1 & 2)	$	$			$
3. HOUSING					
4. FOOD					
5. AUTO					
6. INSURANCE					
7. DEBTS					
8. ENTER/RECREATION					
9. CLOTHING					
10. SAVINGS					
11. INVESTMENTS					
12. MEDICAL					
13. MISCELLANEOUS					
C. TOTALS (3-13 only)	$	$			$
DIFFERENCE (B minus C)	$				

INSTRUCTIONS:
Use pencil. Use nearest dollar amount. Complete column #1 from form #1, column #2 from form #3 and place the difference in column #3. To complete column #4 disregard the (+) and (–) in column #3 and number the differences from the largest difference #1 to the smallest difference #13, **DO NOT** complete column #5 until you have read chapter 7 and completed your new projected budget in the boxes on form #1. When your new projected budget is completed on form #1 then transfer your figures from form #1 to column #5, Form #4 above.

FORM #4

156

Beginning Cash $ ——————
Beginning Checking $ ——————

CURRENT MONTHLY INCOME AND OUTGO RECORD
USE PENCIL — Record every penny daily.

Ending Cash $ ——————
Ending Checking $ ——————

PROJECTED BUDGET → DESCRIPTION OF COLUMNS #1—#12	MONTH / YEAR	1 TITHE (GOD)	2 TAXES (GOV'T.)	3 HOUSING	4 FOOD GROCERY	5 AUTO	6 INSURANCE	7 DEBTS	8 ENTER. REC.	9 CLOTHING	10 SAVINGS	11 INVESTMENTS	12 MEDICAL	13 MISC.	PROJECTED BUDGET DESCRIPTION OF MISC. ONLY #13
GROSS INCOME ALL SOURCES															
	1														
	2														
	3														
	4														
	5														
	6														
	7														
	8														
	9														
	10														
	11														
	12														
	13														
	14														
	15														
	16														
	17														
	18														
	19														
	20														
	21														
	22														
	23														
	24														
	25														
	26														
	27														
	28														
	29														
	30														
	31														
← TOTAL INCOME	MONTHLY TOTALS →						← PROOF TOTALS →								TOTAL OUTGO #1—#13 →
ADD BEGINNING CASH, CHECKS AND TOTAL MONTHLY INCOME										ADD ENDING CASH, CHECKING, TOTAL OUTGO →					
PROJECTED BUDGET LESS MONTHLY TOTALS															

About the Author

MAHLON HETRICK was born in Hershey, Pennsylvania, and lived in Washington, D.C., for twenty-five years. He and his wife, Marlyn, moved to Fort Myers, Florida, in 1959. They have three sons, Gary, Daniel, and Kenneth. Mahlon served in the U.S. Army in Korea, and he is a Dale Carnegie graduate and a graduate of the Savings and Loan School for Executive Development at the University of Georgia. His teaching career includes management, communication, and personal finance courses at Edison Community College and biblical financial counseling at Gulf Shore Christian College and Brethren Biblical Institute.

For many years, Mahlon Hetrick served as a community leader; he is a past president of several organizations. He also served in the church as a deacon, teacher, and finance committee chair, and beyond the church as a past chair of the Christian Businessmen's Committee in Fort Myers.

He has been honored by the Fort Myers Board of Realtors, the Lee County Chamber of

Commerce, and Edison Community College for outstanding service. The National Secretaries Association named him Boss of the Year in 1974–75. After spending most of his thirty years in banking as a senior officer, he founded Christian Financial Counseling, a nonprofit corporation, and serves as its director, senior counselor, and president of the board.

Mahlon counsels with hundreds of counselees per year on a nonfee basis; plus he gives seminars and workshops and serves as a speaker for many groups and organizations, primarily throughout the state of Florida. For several years he has appeared on radio and television talk shows. Hundreds of satisfied counselees refer their friends and family members to Christian Financial Counseling because they have seen God's Word work as it has been compassionately taught by the author. Pastors who have experienced the financial seminars presented by Mahlon have enthusiastically recommended the seminars to other churches.

DIRECT ALL CORRESPONDENCE TO:

Christian Financial Counseling, Inc.
2267 First St. Unit 15
Fort Myers, FL 33901-2954

Phone: (239) 337-2122
Fax: (239) 337-2134
E-mail: Cfcministry7@yahoo.com
Website: www.cfcswf.org